Israel's Unilateralism

Advance Praise for
Israel's Unilateralism:
Beyond Gaza

"Bob Zelnick's study of Israeli unilateralism fills two important needs: for academics, it is a comprehensive initial examination of an issue that will dominate Israeli-Palestinian relations for years to come; and for policy makers, it is a primer on next steps in the peace process. Zelnick's thorough review of Israel's disengagement policy sets the stage for understanding why the consensus within Israel has shifted so dramatically in support of Israeli-Palestinian separation. The extensive interviews conducted by Zelnick add depth and color to this insightful study."

> —Daniel C. Kurtzer, former United States ambassador to Israel and Egypt and the S. Daniel Abraham Visiting Professor of Middle East Policy Studies at Princeton University's Woodrow Wilson School of Public and International Affairs

"Zelnick's book offers the best explanation so far as to how (and why) Israel shifted in recent years towards a policy of unilateralism in pursuing a settlement to its conflict with the Palestinians. It is worthwhile for all students of the Middle East, regardless of where they stand, to read this book, as it offers deep knowledge and great insight into one of the world's most intractable conflicts. If there is a single book that can tell us where Israel stands today and where it is likely to go from here, it is this one."

> —Salameh Nematt, Washington bureau chief for *Al-Hayat* newspaper

"It takes great courage, knowledge, and experience to decipher the complexities of the Israeli-Palestinian relationship. Robert Zelnick displays these qualities in an impressive manner. In *Israel's Unilateralism: Beyond Gaza*, he describes a tremendous paradigm shift, from the hopeful bilateralism of the Oslo years to the uncertain unilateralism of the Gaza pullout and beyond, from integration to separation, from engagement to disengagement. This is a must-read for anyone wishing to know more about the challenges of this conflict."

> —General Mike Herzog, Israel Defense Forces

Israel's Unilateralism
Beyond Gaza

Robert Zelnick

HOOVER INSTITUTION PRESS
Stanford University   Stanford, California

www.hoover.org

Hoover Institution Press Publication No. 550

First printing, 2006
13   12   11   10   09   08   07   06   9   8   7   6   5   4   3   2   1

Manufactured in the United States of America

The paper used in this publication meets the minimum requirements of the American National Standard for Information Sciences—Permanence of Paper for Printed Library Materials, ANSI Z39.48-1992. ∞

Library of Congress Cataloging-in-Publication Data
Zelnick, Bob, 1940–
Israel's unilateralism : beyond Gaza / by Robert Zelnick.
        p.   cm. — (Hoover Institution Press publication ; no. 550)
    Includes bibliographical references and index.
    ISBN 0-8179-4772-8 (alk. paper)
    1. Israel—Politics and government—1993–   2. Gaza Strip—Politics and government.   3. Palestinian Arabs—Attitudes.   4. Jews—Israel—Attitudes.
5. Arab-Israeli conflict—1993—Occupied territories.   6. Sharon, Ariel.
I. Title.   II. Series: Hoover Institution Press publication ; 550.
DS128.2.Z45   2006
956.9405′4—dc22   20060007445

Contents

Acknowledgments   ix

Preface   xiii

1. The Pullout   1

2. Birth of a Doctrine   17

3. Sharon's Surprise   35

4. The Palestinian Moderates   57

5. Hamas and Kin: The Terrorists   77

6. The Settlements   99

7. Politics and Diplomacy   119

8. Unilateralism's Future   141

Index   161

Acknowledgments

This was an exceptionally interesting and rewarding undertaking and my thanks to those who helped make it so are heartfelt. I extend special gratitude to John Raisian, director of the Hoover Institution at Stanford University, for his confidence in this project and for the generous support he provided.

Richard Sousa, Hoover's deputy director, actually came up with the idea over breakfast in Boston. My thanks to Richard; I hope he feels the results approached his expectations.

Dean John Schulz of the Boston University College of Communication supported my travel to and from Israel and was understanding when I needed to work virtually full time on the book in order to present a quality project on deadline. Thanks, John.

My youngest daughter, Marni Ruth Zelnick, a talented second-year graduate film student at NYU, accompanied me on the trip and was vital to its success. She provided excellent background research, recorded and transcribed all interviews where that was possible, got us where we had to go through her uncanny skill interpreting maps, and kept me in great humor throughout the trip. I love her.

I can never express the depth of my gratitude to our old friends, the family of Ruth Beker of Kfar Shmayahu. Ruthie and her son Ehud made sure we were well housed, fed, and equipped. Son Yonatan brought his keen editorial mind to all our conversations and helped arrange some pivotal interviews. We could not have managed anywhere near as well without them, not to mention the wonderful companionship provided by all, including Le-more.

My thanks again go to the Jaffee Center for Strategic Studies in Tel Aviv and its superb director, Zvi Shtauber, for making office space and telephone service available. Thanks too to Research Director Mark Heller for his help with facilities and also an unforgettable Shabat dinner with his delightful family. The Center promotes Israeli-Palestinian dialogue all over Europe, and I'm always surprised at how few U.S. institutions take advantage of its expertise.

Palestinian interviews were critical to the success of the project and no one could have worked harder or more successfully organizing them that Sanad Sahelia, a fine journalist working out of Ramallah. Sanad provided us with one of our biggest laughs of the trip when he interrupted an interview with a Hamas official to urge my daughter to check her Coke bottle cap to see if she had won $10,000.

My thanks to Taghreed El-Khodary, the *New York Times* stringer in Gaza, who arranged travel with a reliable taxi driver, organized several key interviews, and treated me to a delicious lunch during one of my visits to Gaza. When I asked what I could do for her in return, she said she was planning to attend Harvard's Nieman Fellowship Program that fall and would love to have Shabat dinner at our home. Never have I more enjoyed honoring a request.

Back in the States, I wish to thank my colleague Tamar Morad who provided useful research in the areas of Israeli settlements and Palestinian terrorist groups.

Professor Shai Feldman of Brandeis University, presently director of the Crown Center for Middle East Studies and a former director of the Jaffee Center, honored me with invitations to Brandeis events which he knew would be helpful to my work. The generosity and courtesy he displayed went a long way towards making this a better book; for this I am deeply grateful. And although the Crown Center itself is a new center for scholarship, it is well on its way to making a major contribution to the field.

Thanks to David Makovsky of the Washington Institute for Near East Policy, author of a fine book, *Engagement Through Disengagement*, for sharing his wisdom with me.

General Mike Herzog of IDF, a visiting fellow at the above-mentioned Washington Institute, provided keen insight before I left for Israel and read an early manuscript of this book, critiquing it over a period of four hours on a fine mid-January day. This was truly service "above and beyond," and I think Mike knows the depth of my appreciation.

Joshua Itzkowitz Shifrinson, an undergraduate at Brandeis, did an absolutely fantastic job proofing, editing, fact-checking, footnoting, and generally doing everything humanly possible to make this a better piece of work. He is a talented young man who will one day make a very big mark in the world of scholarship.

My gratitude too to those who helped on this project but, for good reason, requested not to be named.

Special thanks to my Boston University assistant, Sheryl Jackson Holliday, for helping to "cover" for me for a period of weeks after classes resumed in January.

And, to my wife of thirty-eight years, Pamela, for adapting with tolerance and love to the screwy work habits of her husband.

Preface

The day after the stunning Hamas victory of January 24, a number of calls from friends and colleagues expressed their condolences. Their voices were hushed, empathetic, suitable for a bereavement occasion, which I guess they thought it was. First Sharon and now this! Could your luck have been any worse? Do you still have a book left? Oh, I feel so badly for you.

Well, dry those tears, folks. The editorial casket is still empty. Woe be unto the author who writes a book that chases the headlines as opposed to merely taking them into account as one would any other new source of information. In those hollow months between submission and publication, the headlines will always catch and pass the narrative.

Not so with a book about a strategy, in this case unilateral separation. It was designed by strategic thinkers—both military and civilian—to address a situation where the status quo was unacceptable, where negotiated change was to be preferred, but where that prospect was rendered unobtainable by the absence of a negotiating partner on the other side. The proffered solution was to implement the desired changes unilaterally and to undertake defensive measures to prevent any corresponding degradation of security. In its first stage, this meant total Israeli withdrawal from Gaza, symbolic withdrawal from four West Bank settlements, and construction of a security fence to keep suicide bombers and other terrorists at bay.

The purpose of the move was essentially demographic. There

were too many Palestinians and too few Israelis living on land controlled by Israel. Gaza was an extreme example of this situation, with eight thousand Jews and 1.3 million Arabs living in close proximity. To preserve both the Jewish and democratic character of the Israeli state, a withdrawal was needed. Eventually, the logic goes, the combination of tearing down settlements far from the borders of pre-1967 Israel and building a security fence around the country's new perimeter would come to define the permanent borders of Israel.

This strategy was adopted by Prime Minister Ariel Sharon—originally a skeptic—vis-à-vis a Palestinian government totally controlled by the actions (or lack thereof) of the discredited Yasser Arafat and his Fatah political party. The withdrawal was executed after Arafat's death and his replacement by Mahmoud Abbas (Abu Mazen), an opponent of the Second Intifada. However, though he is, by all accounts, a good and decent man, he is also something of a ninety-seven-pound political weakling.

Fatah, meanwhile, with its Intifada treachery and out-of-control militias, was still a fair distance from being judged negotiation-eligible. Yet compared to Hamas—with its charter-based commitment to the eradication of Israel and slaughter of Jews—it was positively benign. Most Israelis, their American backers, and even their European associates were sorry to see Hamas win the January 2006 legislative council elections. The strategy of unilateral disengagement, however, is more applicable to a Hamas-led Palestinian government than it was to a Fatah government with whom Road Map negotiations would probably have begun within a matter of months. If one may venture a prediction, unilateral Israeli actions affecting both land and security will become the norm for dealing with the Palestinians in the wake of the January 2006 elections and continue so long as Hamas is both in power and committed to its present objectives.

My first brush with the strategy of unilateral disengagement came during the bleak summer of 2002 when suicide bombers were doing their bloody work in many of Israel's major cities. A left-of-center academic who was, when I first met him in the mid-1980s, a foe of Israeli West Bank settlements, argued that Israel could not leave it to terrorists to define the kind of state it is. It has no business imposing itself on five and one-half million Palestinians as you then get into the business of perennial suppression, bad news for a democracy. On the other hand, Israel has always been able to protect its borders against Egypt, Jordan, and Syria; Israeli defense was strong irrespective of the given enemy. Thus, one did not need to occupy their people to attain one's goals. Pull back, put up a fence, keep your military options open, and you will have both security and demography working for you.

I did not like the idea at first because it fell between negotiating a complete, internationally recognized and secure accord or—another effective remedy—bashing the stuffing out of the people who attack you. This would look like an Israeli retreat. Terrorists would be emboldened. Or, worse yet, opportunities to achieve a real negotiating breakthrough would be fatally undermined.

Yet I could not resist the opportunity to come back and see for myself how the withdrawal from Gaza was working, its searing effect upon the religious Zionists, its role in the self-rediscovery of the country's political center, the judgment of Palestinians of several political persuasions (including Hamas), and the views of many of Israel's rising political stars, including Deputy—now Acting—Prime Minister Ehud Olmert and Minister of Justice—now Foreign Minister—Tsipi Livni. Where possible without compromising the flow of the narrative, as well as to do justice to the original intentions of this work, I let their comments run long enough for the reader to get a feel for the texture as well as the substance of their remarks

My approach, as you might guess, is half academic and half

journalistic. I begin chapter 1 with an account of the actual pull-out from Gaza and the frustrated efforts by Orthodox Jewish supporters from the West Bank settlements who tried to come to the settlers' aid. In chapter 2, I deal with the evolution of the idea of unilateral disengagement, a concept which actually grew from Israeli efforts to picture what a negotiated resolution of border differences might look like if negotiations were successful.

Sharon, the former "Bulldozer" of the settlement movement, was the indispensable party to the new policy and I devote chapter 3 to his metamorphosis. His illness, though tragic, nonetheless presented Israeli voters with the chance to reject or institutionalize the doctrine during a political campaign without Sharon's daunting presence. Truly this campaign was interpreted by all parties as a referendum on unilateral withdrawal from much of the West Bank. When he does develop a comprehensive plan, Olmert may not have to seek approval outside the Knesset.

Chapter 4 gives the beleaguered Palestinian moderates their moment in the sun. Then in chapters 5 and 6, I isolate Palestinian terrorism and Israeli settlement policies at some length as each represents the fundamental grievance of each side with the other and deserves independent examination. With Hamas now in the Palestinian saddle, both issues become even more important as both Israel and the U.S. say there can be no talks with Hamas until it renounces terrorism even as Hamas maintains it will not relent in its commitment to destroy Israel until Israel returns to the 1967 borders.

In chapter 7, I look at the exceptionally active and important period of politics and diplomacy that resulted from the Gaza pull-out, including the collapse of Abu Mazen's efforts to both placate and neutralize Hamas and Sharon's venture to translate Gaza into improved international standing and, finally, his push to form a new centrist party, Kadima (Forward). Kadima's victory, in a closer-than-anticipated vote, left open the question of whether the

Kadima Party, the policy of nationalism, or both can now stand alone without the protective hulk of Sharon in the picture. I then conclude with chapter 8, summarizing where disengagement has been, where it may go in the future under given conditions, and underscore the politically realist-minded assumptions that continue to drive the policy forward.

Like Sharon, I have come a long way on unilateral disengagement without becoming in any sense blind to its limitations. A wily terrorist does not belong at the negotiating table. Still, his absence need not define the nature of Israeli society or the boundaries of the Israeli state, and it is with this assumption in mind that I approach the material.

ISRAEL
WEST BANK
GAZA STRIP
Mediterranean Sea
Beit Hanoun (Erez) Crossing
Al-Atatra
Beit Lahiya
Shati RC
Jabalya RC
Gaza
Planned Gaza Seaport
Nezarim
An-Nuseirat RC
Al-Mintar (Karni) Crossing
Bureij RC
Deir Al Balah RC
GAZA STRIP
Al-Maghazi RC
Kfar Darom
ISRAEL
Katif
Ganei Tal
Kissufim Crossing
Neve Dekalim
Khan Yunis
Bedolah
Morag
Rafah
Planned Industrial Zone
Sufa Crossing
EGYPT
Gaza Airport
International Boundary
Armistice Line, 1949
District Boundary
Settlement access road patrolled by Israel
Palestinian cities, localities and Refugee Camps, (RC)
Israeli settlements
10 Km
10 Miles

Source: Information provided by Palestinian Academic Society for the Study of International Affairs, Map Resources. Adapted by CRS. (K. Yancey 1/13/05)

1. The Pullout

ON A WARM MID-AUGUST NIGHT, an estimated thirty to forty thousand Israeli civilians converged upon the northern Negev desert town of Netivot as a convoy of buses ferried them to what would become the critical front in their battle to halt Israel's military evacuation of the Gaza Strip and the dismemberment of twenty-one settlements located there. Their plan was to mobilize at Netivot, surge on foot to nearby Kfar Maimon serving as a staging area for a rush to a checkpoint called Kissufim, and then on to the largest and most significant settlement bloc in the Gaza Strip, Gush Katif. With tens of thousands of committed foes of withdrawal firmly planted in Gaza, the logic was that neither the police mobilized for the evacuation nor their Israeli Defense Force (IDF) allies would be able to execute their orders. The plan of the traitorous Prime Minister, Ariel Sharon, would be thwarted. So confident of success were the demonstration's leaders, they had only chartered the busses for a one-way trip. The return rides, weeks or months into the future, could be organized at a later date.

Many in the anti-evacuation crowd wore orange T-shirts, shorts, trousers, or frocks, borrowing the official color from the local Gush Katif council. Most of those dressed in more traditional colors still wore orange ribbons, wristbands or laces. The majority of riders were residents not of Gaza but of settlements among the approximately 140 located in Judea and Samaria, what most of the world refers to as the West Bank. Nearly all the men and boys wore skullcaps, with cords of thread (*tsitsis*) hanging below shirt bottoms. These were religious Zionists, followers of Rabbi Avram Yitzhak Kook, chief rabbi during the pre-statehood period, and his son, Rabbi Tsvi Yehudah Cook, who held the same post years after 1948.

To the elder Rabbi Cook goes credit for developing the doctrine of religious Zionism during the 1930s, thereby breaking the near monopoly of the secular Zionists on the sociology of the nascent state. Devout Zionist Jews are vastly different from some of the Hassidic orthodox, the Haredi, who see Israel as a secular fraud, decline to serve in its military, and believe the faithful must spend their time preparing for the Messiah, whose visit will usher in the true state of Israel. The Zionist orthodox, on the other hand, dedicate themselves to working through the state to help bring about conditions conducive to the Messiah's arrival. In Rabbi Avram Yitzhak Kook's words, "The State of Israel is the foundation of God's throne on earth."[1]

If the elder Rabbi Kook helped define *what* Israel is, then Rabbi Tsvi Yehudah Kook tried to define *where* it is. Following the Six Days' War of 1967, when Israel conquered the West Bank, the Sinai, and the Golan Heights, the younger Rabbi Kook pronounced the results symbolic of God's will that the entire biblical Land of Israel remain in Jewish hands. Thus did the concept of Greater Israel take hold and adherents of religious Zionism become the backbone of the West Bank settlers' movement. Their political and self-governing arm, the Yesha Council—Yesha being a Hebrew acronym for Judea, Samaria and Gaza—led the opposition to the Gaza disengagement plan. Notably, the council's most powerful ally at the time was the more extreme Bayit Leumi (National Home) organization, many of whose members favored outright dispossession of resident Palestinians.

1. Rabbi Dov Begon, "Vayishlach: No Longer Jacob," *Arutz Sheva*, December 14, 2005.

The intensity of devout Zionist fervor has been explained by the important role settlement has come to play in overcoming decades-old feelings of inferiority with respect to both secular Israelis and the Hassidim; historically, religious Zionists could not match the nation-building activities of the former or the religious scholarship of the latter. As Professor Avi Ravitsky of the Institute of Jewish Studies at the Hebrew University of Jerusalem told the newspaper *Haaretz,* "Clinging to settlement of the land solved both of these problems. We are both *building* the land and are devout. This gave an entire generation its identity, and now they are going to take this identity away from it. It is being told: You are being defeated by history."[2]

The religious Zionists also serve in the military in numbers disproportionate to their share of the population. By virtue of an agreement with the government, students from their *yeshivot hesder* (religious schools) commit themselves to military service for sixteen months, after which they can return to their schools to complete their studies over a thirty-two-month period while remaining eligible for further service in the event of a reserve call-up.[3] In this, they are part of what Israelis describe as a "religious revolution" within the IDF. The secular collective farming communities—the kibbutzim and moshavim—have long since become too sparse to satisfy the lion's share of IDF manpower needs. In addition, many of those from secular backgrounds have had difficulty reconciling their moral and political views with service in places like Gaza, the West Bank, and Lebanon. The religious have filled the void. Mostly they are trained for army tank and infantry service and many were on active duty over the summer of 2005, assigned to the units charged with enforcing the evacuation. Reflecting the events of the pullout from Gaza (to be discussed be-

2. Yair Sheleg, "The Insult of Religious Zionism," *Haaretz,* July 25, 2005.
3. Amos Harel, "Countdown for D-Day (Reexamining the Hesder Arrangement)," *Haaretz Special Magazine,* August 15, 2005.

low), the IDF let it be known that it was rethinking the role of mixed units versus those reflected by the yeshivot hesder units.

The Yesha Council took account but not full advantage of the changing composition of the IDF and never formulated a coherent political strategy for addressing such soldiers. As a result, rabbis and other leaders were free to follow individual instincts. A handful of the more extreme rabbis urged soldiers to disobey military orders to dislodge settlers. Others simply pleaded with the military to be tolerant of soldiers who felt they could not in conscience execute the order to evacuate the Gaza settlements, forcefully if necessary. Adi Mintz, former Yesha Council CEO and still a reservist, had told his reserve unit to go on without him. Still smarting in his Lod office just days before the first planned evacuation from what he regarded as a betrayal by Sharon, Mintz said he thought there was a chance the army would disintegrate under the burden of its task. "I hope that the commanders of the army will understand people like me who cannot do it, orders like this," he said. "I think that this order is immoral. I think that this is dangerous to the people of Israel. I think that this order is against all the Zionist movement." Yet he added that whatever the outcome in Gaza, the nation had to continue living together as one people, and that meant no violence. "In all our demonstrations we have told our people not to use violence," he added. "It is a very, very important point to us during all our demonstrations. All the people in the Yesha Council think like me. Not all of the people in the settlements, but all of the people in the Council."[4]

It had, in fact, been an act of violence that led to the settlers' first defeat in July with the forced evacuation of the Maoz Yam hotel at Gush Katif. In the early spring, outside settler sympathizers began infiltrating into the hotel, hoping to eventually attract numbers large and aggressive enough to resist evacuation.

4. Adi Mintz, transcript of interview with author, Lod, August 7, 2005.

But a stone-throwing incident in which a Palestinian boy was allegedly lynched by the outsiders led security forces to clear the hotel a month ahead of schedule. The task took about fifteen minutes, a strong indication that evacuating Jewish militants from their fortresses of choice might turn out to be less difficult than imagined.

Stopping the human rush to Gush Katif in July was a combined military and police operation of about twenty thousand, one of the largest of its kind in Israel's history. Security officials were divided as to where to draw the line. Police Lieutenant Commander Nisso Shaham, serving as Police commander of the Negev region, wanted the buses carrying protesters halted on the roads and turned back to their points of origin even before reaching Netivot, an idea endorsed by Police Major General Yohanan Danino. On the other hand, Police Commissioner Moshe Karadi argued that citizens in a free society should be allowed to express their views. He maintained that the Yesha Council should be told that the police could tolerate a rally at Netivot and a procession to Kfar Maimon so long as the demonstrators made no effort to march to Gush Katif in Gaza. That way the rally would create only a minor "breach of order." Moving into Gush Katif would be a flagrant "breach of law."

The debate became academic when Dudi Cohen, director of Police Intelligence and Communications, confirmed that rally organizers had purchased only one-way tickets aboard the 650 buses hauling the demonstrators, conclusive evidence that they intended to remain at Gush Katif for an extended period. The commanders changed their plans abruptly. Now security forces were told to intercept and turn back as many of the buses as they could prevent from reaching Netivot. No one could know with precision the number of settlers who never made it to the tiny desert town but guesses ranged to the tens of thousands. Those who did press on to their destination conducted their rally and then marched to Kfar Maimon where most encamped for the night, confident that the morrow would find them in Gush Katif as the leading wedge of a campaign of civil disobedience that would defeat the Gaza pullout.[5]

They were mistaken. That night, IDF forces and police under Southern District commander Uri Bar-Lev surrounded the sleeping minions and, at daybreak, prevented them from moving toward the Kissufim checkpoint. They were trapped at Kfar Maimon, described by one *Haaretz* reporter as "an isolated site that is difficult to access and is surrounded by fences." Infuriated and offended, the demonstrators lashed out verbally at the soldiers, calling them "traitor," and even "Nazi."[6] But to no avail. The line of soldiers—often a big circle with hands joined, rotating around the demonstrators—held. As the day became hot, the ranks of settlers began to thin. Permitted to walk through the line of military personnel in groups of twos and threes, many could be seen on cell phones talking to friends and relatives who had stayed behind, trying now to organize transportation back to the West Bank, their one-way buses having long since departed. To all intents and purposes, the battle to save Gush Katif (so it could be destroyed) ended before it began: with protestors turned back, the residents were left with few tools at their disposal, solely able to evoke human sympathy as the victims of a lost cause.

This was evident a few days later when the disengagement foes mobilized in the Negev development town of Sderot, a regional mini-hub and a harder place to isolate, for what could have been a second effort to reach Gaza. Instead, leaders of the Yesha Council met with security forces before the event and agreed to march only to nearby Ofakim, just outside the entrance to Gaza. Rather than firing up the crowd, the speeches at Sderot seemed

5. See Amir Oren, "Democracy in Action," *Haaretz,* July 22, 2005, for a complete account of the confrontation at Kfar Maimon.
6. Ibid.

more like policy statements intended to run long enough to give the many late-arriving buses a chance to disgorge their passengers.

This time, few insults and epithets were hurled at the security forces. Instead, the largely orthodox group—most accompanied by wives and many by infants and toddlers—broke into chants of camaraderie with those keeping them out of Gaza. "*Hayal, shoter, any ohev otcha,*" they chanted. (Soldier, Policeman, I love you.) "*Hayal, shoter, haim ata ochev oti?*" (Soldier, Policeman, do you love me?) Yesha Council leaders raced alongside the marchers urging good behavior. No attempt to get to Gaza, they reminded the marchers. Please keep in mind that our march ends in Ofakim.[7] That would be the last big event in the desert.

The change in tone was not entirely random. High-level backstage talks between police, IDF commanders, and rabbis associated with the settler movement had established mutually respected ground rules for the events. Also, in preparatory evacuation discussions with the settlers and to assist authorities during the desert confrontations, the IDF had dispatched members of its Special Negotiation team. Formed in the early 1970s to deal with hostage taking and other terrorist incidents, the team was now tasked for the first time to handle highly emotional, sometimes hysterical Israelis who had put their lives into the settlements and now felt themselves abandoned. From all reports these IDF teams, advised by psychiatrists accompanying them to the settlements, contributed to the success of the operation. So did a substantial representation of female soldiers from the Special Negotiatinig unit assigned to deal with women settlers and their children.

The government also showed it could contain the damage from two nightmare incidents, the murders of eight Palestinian

7. Author, as witnessed at Sderot Rally, August 2, 2005.

civilians by fanatical Israeli settlers in two incidents occurring two weeks apart. The first took place in the Druze Galilee town of Shfaram when Eden Natan-Zada, a military deserter, opened fire aboard a bus, killing four non-Jewish Israelis, including two sisters returning from school. The killer was subsequently overpowered by local police, handcuffed, and then beaten to death by the irate crowd while the police scampered to safety. Sharon immediately branded the shooting "a heinous act by a blood-thirsty terrorist" and was clever enough to note that the victims were also "Israeli citizens."[8] A few days later he was pictured offering condolences to the father of the two murdered girls. An interfaith delegation of Jews, Christians and Muslims called on the aggrieved families to offer condolences. An announced plan to investigate those responsible for Natan-Zada's death was quietly dropped.

Two weeks later and just days after the evacuation at Gush Katif had begun, a settler shot and killed four Palestinian workers at the industrial zone in the settlement of Shiloh. The murderer, Asher Weissgan, lived in the settlement of Shvut Rahel, many of whose residents tend to follow the militant leadership of Rabbi Moshe Levinger. Several such followers have allegedly been involved in acts of violence and intimidation of nearby Palestinian villages. Once again Sharon was quick to condemn "this Jewish terror attack, aimed at innocent Palestinians out of a warped belief that this would prevent the disengagement plan." Sharon's senior advisor, Dov Weissglas, phoned President Mahmoud Abbas' top assistant to apologize and Abbas quickly issued a statement urging Palestinians not to retaliate.[9] Like the Shfaram killings, the Shiloh murders quickly disappeared from the front pages

---

8. Aluf Benn, Eli Ashkenazi, and Jonathan Lis, "Jewish Soldier Kills 4 Israeli Arabs in Shfaram; Angry Mob Beats Him to Death," *Haaretz*, August 5, 2005.

9. Haaretz Correspondents and Agencies, "Sharon Slams Jewish Terror Attack," *Haaretz*, August 18, 2005.

with few apparent repercussions. In both cases the families of the dead received compensation from a special government fund reserved for the victims of terrorism.

As the August 15 deadline for the first evacuations approached, the Yesha Council staged massive events at the Wailing Wall and Rabin Square in Tel Aviv, drawing crowds in the hundreds of thousands but, according to the polls, changing few minds. A steady majority of 55–60 percent of Israelis favored the pullout, and while the number of demonstrators was impressive, the rallies at times tended to resemble stops on a bus tour for religious West Bank settlers, many of the same ones appearing at each "performance."[10] Their speakers continued to passionately condemn the violation of the principle tracing back to pre-statehood days that "Jews don't expel Jews." Many continued to believe the withdrawal would never occur. Some were led to that conclusion by their rabbis. Mordecai Eliyahu, for example, chief rabbi of the Sefardi community, contemplated the withdrawal and concluded "it is not going to happen." Many of his followers echoed those words. Yet their assessments sounded more and more unworldly. Here on earth—or at least that sandy patch of it—the IDF and cooperating law enforcement agencies were in control.

Inside Gaza, perhaps half of the eight thousand Jewish settlers—including nearly all the secular ones—were already gone, having accepted government relocation assistance which was later extended to the recalcitrants as well. Those who remained attracted enormous national and international attention.[11] In just

10. Agence France Presse—English, "Most Israelis Support Gaza Withdrawal: Poll," *Agence France Presse*, July 18, 2005; UPI Correspondents, "Israelis' Support for Pullback Increases," *UPI*, July 1, 2005; and UPI Correspondents, "Smaller Majority Still Favors Pullouts," *UPI*, June 10, 2005.

11. Greg Myre, Steven Erlanger, and Dina Kraft, "Thousands Hold Out in Gaza Against Evacuation," *New York Times*, August 15, 2005.

two days, seventeen soldiers per housing unit would make sure the Gush Katif settlers were removed. Homes, rejected by the Palestinians as too small and with too few rooms for their large families, would be demolished by the departing Israelis. The synagogues would be left standing until the Palestinians turned them to rubble. Torah scrolls would be lovingly removed. The remains of the dead would be disinterred for reburial on Jewish soil.

Some reporting missed important nuances of the story. For example, many journalists covering the pullout paid considerable attention to the fate of four thousand greenhouses which had generated about $120 million a year in flowers and agricultural revenue for the Israelis. At first blush it seemed like a bonanza for the economically pressed Palestinians. A closer look, however, suggested greater complexity. As he assessed Gaza's economic prospects on the balcony of a large hotel overlooking the sea, Salah Abed Shafi, a Palestinian Authority economic planner, said the wealth generated by the Israeli greenhouses would be difficult to transfer.[12] The problem was not how to grow things but how to sell and transport them to market, particularly with travel restrictions and impediments imposed by the Israelis in the name of security. "We have at least twelve thousand greenhouses," Abed Shafi said. "Sixty percent of production cannot be marketed. Now to add another four thousand greenhouses with no guarantee for marketing—it would be a burden."[13] In the end, political negotiations arranged for private donations to compensate the Israelis and let the Palestinians keep the greenhouses on the chance they would be of some utility.

JEWS LIVED IN GAZA in biblical times, but it was modern Israel's first prime minister, David Ben Gurion, who urged the formation

12. Salah Abed Shafi, transcript of interview with author, Gaza, July 30, 2005.
13. Ibid.

of settlements in Gaza; Kfar Darom, in 1946, became the first. Yet this first wave of settlement proved tenuous and a 1948 Egyptian siege forced the abandonment of Kfar Darom and an Israeli withdrawal from the area as a whole until the late 1960s and early 1970s. At that time, Israel was able to use its victory in the Six Days' War of 1967 to renew settlement efforts, resettling Kfar Darom in 1970 and transforming army outposts at Netzarim and Morag into settlements in 1972. A subsequent boost to Israeli settlement in Gaza came as a result of the 1981 peace treaty with Egypt when Egyptian president Anwar Sadat declined to reinherit the territory, which then held some three-quarters of a million Palestinians, a majority of them refugees living in festering camps. He did, however, insist on a complete Israeli withdrawal from the Sinai, including those facilities Israeli settlers had built at Yamit. To make room for the former Yamit residents and others, the Israelis began a new wave of Gaza settlement construction—more than a dozen Gaza settlements were constructed after the Egypt-Israel peace accord. In time, some Israelis would be ejected twice by their government, once from Yamit and again from their "permanent" residences in Gaza.

Over the years, the settlements were deployed with strategic objectives in mind. For example, the Gush Katif bloc of sixteen settlements along the southern Gaza coast could impede access from the large Palestinian cities of Rafah and Khan Yunis either to the Egyptian border or the coast. The other settlement, on the northern end of the Strip, helped extend the Israeli presence from Ashkelon on the southern Israeli coast to the edges of Gaza City. Isolated Kfar Darom is on a north-south axis in the heart of the Gaza Strip and was intended primarily to separate Palestinian population centers while serving as an Israeli transportation corridor. Unlike many of the West Bank settlements, particularly those adjacent to towns and villages populated by Palestinians, the initiative for the Gaza settlements came from the government with terms more generous than settlers could find elsewhere. They were, in effect, offered a compact for life.

Yet as time would tell, the offer was a ruse. "Every Israeli prime minister since 1967 has wanted to get rid of Gaza," a senior western diplomat observed. "In any negotiation, from Begin to Barak, it was first item on the table."[14] Tsipi Livni, the minister of justice who supported Prime Minister Sharon's decision to evacuate Gaza and later left the Likud with him, offered a similar analysis:

> I have some sessions with some of my friends, I don't like this name, but the Rebels. They say they are totally against this and I say, "But do you not understand that at the end of the day there is the need to do something, to compromise, to give some of the land?" They say, "Yes." I say, "So now we are talking about tactical issues. It's not ideology."[15]

In the first place, the peace treaty with Egypt nullified part of the strategic justification for an Israeli presence in Gaza. Second and vastly more important were the demographics of the territory. Despite nearly forty years of settlement activity only about eight thousand Jews had chosen to reside there, compared to more than 1.3 million Palestinian residents and refugees. Between the settlements, agricultural areas, roads and the Erez industrial zone, Israeli settlers occupied just over 20 percent of the land area. The population density of that area was 123 people per square km. In the Palestinian areas it was 4,362, among the most densely populated patches of land on earth.[16]

14. Interview with senior western diplomat, July 22, 2005. Two senior western diplomats were interviewed during the course of research; both requested anonymity and their names are withheld per mutual agreement.

15. Tsipi Livni, transcript of interview with author, Jerusalem, August 14, 2005. Note that Tsipi Livni was also appointed minister of foreign affairs on January 18, 2006.

16. Peace Now, "Disengagement—Profiling the Settlements," *Settlements in Focus: Vol. 1, Issue 5*, July 8, 2005 at www.peacenow.org/briefs; The World Bank,

The numbers understated the physical differences between the two populations. The settlements were prim, spacious, pleasant communities where, according to one sensitive observer, residents worried about Palestinian rocket attacks but left their keys in the ignitions of cars parked casually on the streets. The homes ranged up to six bedrooms. Swimming pools were community fixtures. In the Gush Katif bloc, teenagers would scramble over dunes to surf and swim. The sea was a common heritage. Nearly all the fresh water in Gaza was under Israel's control. But because of the declining aquifer, water for Gaza must daily be piped in from Israel.

Israeli agriculture and industry provided work for about ten thousand Gaza residents. Before the outbreak of violence in 2000, tens of thousands of Gazans found work in Israel each day. With employment in Israel restricted after the eruption of the Second Intifada, local Palestinian unemployment easily exceeded 50 percent. A majority of the population, moreover, were refugees and the descendents of refugees from pre-1948 Palestine, caught in a vice of Israeli settlement activity and a cynical Arab policy of preserving the Palestinian "right of return" to Israel by preventing their resettlement anywhere else. The refugee camps were squalid, overpacked affairs where radical politics flourished, providing a rich popular base for terrorist recruitment. The bigger cities—Gaza, Khan Younis, Rafah—were dusty and pulsing, dangerous places where members of armed gangs and clans could be seen along streets while vendors hawked their goods and wildly careening taxis narrowly missed teenagers scurrying to and from market in carts drawn by horses or donkeys.

Stagnation or Revival? Israeli Disengagement and Palestinian Economic Prospects, December 2004 and "Annex: Disengagement, the Palestinian Economy, and Settlements," June 2, 2004; and United States Central Intelligence Agency, "The Gaza Strip," *C.I.A. World Factbook,* November 1, 2005. Data on the population of the Gaza Strip is available from the Israeli Central Bureau of Statistics at www.cbs.gov.il/mifkad/e-mifk.htm.

To many Israelis, Gaza was dysfunctional. It had been fenced off from the rest of the country for a decade. Meanwhile, Hamas and other terrorist groups provided a threat almost exclusively to the Jews who lived there and the soldiers needed to protect them. According to IDF figures cited by the *Jerusalem Post*, in the settlement of Neve Dekalin, one out of five homes had taken a direct hit from missiles, mortars, or gunfire since the Second Intifada began in October of 2000. During the same period, Gaza's Jewish communities had suffered more than 14,790 attacks by automatic weapons, mortars, Qassam missiles, infiltrations, anti-tank rockets, and car bombs. The attacks killed 149 soldiers and civilians.[17]

More than half the Gaza settlers and nearly all of those from four small West Bank settlements also slated for evacuation had moved out by August 17, the day involuntary withdrawal began. Still, many religious Jews of Gaza, encouraged by their rabbis, expected deliverance. God would not countenance Jews removing Jews from the Land of Israel. In the end, the *hesder* soldiers would not enforce the decree. Those who settled His land could show their faith by continuing to live normally, going about their business as though all would be well. Many did, planting flowers and sewing agricultural seeds that would not bloom for months, continuing with lesson plans at *yeshivot*, changing light bulbs, painting rooms, making small repairs associated with continuity. Still there were reports of last-minute resistance. Despite the security, one official estimate proclaimed that as many as five to six thousand protesters had infiltrated the settlements to put up a last ditch battle with the evacuation forces.[18] Some of the newcomers hastily put together wooden shacks, a symbolic gesture of solidarity with the settlers but one that proved little more than nui-

17. C. Robert Zelnick, "The Gaza Pullout," *Boston Phoenix*, September 9, 2005.

18. Guy Raz, "Israelis Begin to Leave Gaza Settlements," CNN Live Sunday, CNN Transcripts, August 14, 2004, 17:00 ET at cnn.com.

sance value to the soldiers. Another report had hundreds of teen-age protesters preparing an act of mass suicide, paddling their surf boards out to sea until wave and exhaustion carried them to their doom.[19] The plan evaporated like drizzle in the desert.

In the end there were tears and embraces, but only one incident involving serious violence. At the religious settlement of Kfar Darom, an acid-like substance, along with paint and eggs, was thrown at advancing IDF troops. There were forty-four injuries, none critical.[20] The soldiers, some with skullcaps instead of helmets and some with both, obeyed their orders. So did most settlers, with many turning their homes into rubble at the last minute less the dwellings fall into non-Jewish hands. Television crews captured it all. Print journalists found families who had lost loved ones to terrorist attacks "defending" their homes against the IDF, children who watched Ima and Abba shed tears of grief and resignation. In barely a week the twenty-one Gaza settlements and four on the West Bank were gone. Gaza, geographically identical to its pre-1967 contours, was returned to the Palestinians. By contrast, few settlements were abandoned in Samaria and the IDF remained in control on the ground.

Gush Etzion is a settlement bloc of thirty thousand in the mountains north of Jerusalem. One day in August 2005, Shaul Goldstein rose from his chair in the business office at Gush Etzion, moved to a large window, and pointed to what appeared to be a filmy white line painted across the bottom of a very distant horizon. "You see the horizon there—that white line on the horizon is Tel Aviv," he said. "From the white line to this quarry here—this is Israel." His voice rose with emotion: "And they want us to give away from this quarry to the Jordan River, and this is very,

19. Nadav Shragai, "Gush Katif Surfer Teens Threaten Group Suicide on the Waves," *Haaretz*, August 8, 2005.

20. Yuval Azoulay, "44 Hurt, 150 Held in Kfar Darom Synagogue Clashes," *Haaretz*, August 19, 2005.

very dangerous. The purpose is to weaken Israel. And after they have weakened Israel, they will start another war with another excuse, the right of return."[21]

Goldstein, whose father fought unsuccessfully to capture La-trun from Jordanian forces during Israel's War of Independence, was speaking a week before the Gaza pullout. He thought the political trend was favorable, shrinking support for unilateral disengagement among Israel's Jews. He said political mistakes had been made by the religious leadership in failing to unite politically with secular forces who opposed the pullout on security grounds. But they had learned from their mistakes. Bigger battles lay ahead.

Judea and Samaria would be different, he vowed. Very different.

21. Shaul Goldstein, transcript of interview with author, Gush Etzion, August 7, 2005.

2. Birth of a Doctrine

FEW REMEMBER: The new era in the Middle East began at 6: 45 A.M. on September 29, 2000, when a Palestinian policeman, Na'il Suileiman, got out of the Palestinian jeep that was taking part in a joint patrol with Israel in Qalqilyah, walked over to the Israeli jeep and shot his Israeli counterpart, Yossi Tabeja, a Border Policeman, at point-blank range.[1]

The writer of this retrospective vignette, Ari Shavit of *Haaretz*, recalls the joint patrol as an icon of the Oslo period. Thus, its demise is a fitting symbol of the demise of everything associated with the 1993 deal, namely, mutual recognition, a rejection of violence, the peaceful resolution of the four "final status" issues—borders, settlements, Jerusalem, and refugees.

Others might have picked different moments. One might select October 12, 2000, when two Israeli soldiers were lynched by a Palestinian mob after erroneously entering Ramallah.[2] Or perhaps March 27, 2002 when a suicide bomber killed thirty Jews enjoying their Passover Seder at the Park Hotel in Netanya, triggering Prime Minister Ariel Sharon's decision to reoccupy Palestinian cities from which Israeli security forces had withdrawn pur-

---

1. Ari Shavit, "So Mature, This New Israeli Majority," *Haaretz Special Magazine,* August 15, 2005.
2. Margot Dudkevitch and Arieh O'Sullivan, "Israel Launches Reprisal Attacks on PA for 2 Soldiers Lynched in Ramallah," *Jerusalem Post*, October 13, 2000.

suant to the Oslo II agreement (dubbed Operation Defensive Shield).[3]

In tracing the path of unilateral disengagement and Sharon's ultimate embrace of the doctrine, such searing and spectacular incidents can either illuminate underlying trends or blind the observer to these dynamics. The initial planning for the geographic separation of Israelis and Palestinians came during the administration of Prime Minister Ehud Barak (1999–2001) and was predicated on the assumption that talks with the Palestinians would succeed. In other words, separation would be part of a comprehensive agreement on borders. Barak accordingly launched a series of interdepartmental studies under the direction of Shaul Arieli, head of his "Peace Administration." Another strong presence was Transport Minister Ephraim Sneh. Both urged the prime minister to initiate the program with or without a deal with the Palestinians, advice Barak ignored. Instead, even after the failure at Camp David, he continued his talks with the PA as the Second Intifada began and his political standing crumbled. Their failure destroyed the political mandate of Barak's Labor government and brought Sharon's hard-line Likud-led coalition to power.[4]

Many political observers would cite the massive violence and virulent anti-Israeli sentiment on display during "Intifada 2" as the best indications that the real objective of the Palestinians was eradication of the Jewish state. This view was reinforced as accounts of the last gasp "Clinton Parameters" and final Taba burial ceremony of December 2000 and January 2001 came to light. Taba came about after President Bill Clinton, moving more quietly but no less dramatically than he had previously at Camp David (July 2000), sought to rescue the negotiation process from col-

3. Karin Laub, "Israeli Top Officials Meet Amid Calls for Retaliation After Suicide Attack Kills 20," *Associated Press*, March 28, 2002.

4. Leslie Susser, "Time to Build the Fence?" *Jerusalem Report*, August 27, 2001.

lapse by defining the "parameters" for resolving outstanding issues. Taba would then underline the fact that deep and fundamental differences on key issues had never been bridged since
the start of the Oslo process. In the public relations battle to follow, largely over which side or individual bore primary responsibility for the failure of the talks and return to violence, the overall picture of systemic failure became blurred.

An important source detailing the difficulties was the "Moratinos Document," compiled by European Union envoy Miguel
Moratinos from notes he and members of his staff assembled after
conferring with negotiators from both sides following closed door
bargaining sessions.[5] Even as members of each team praised the
atmosphere inside the meeting rooms, they charted fundamental
differences on many critical issues. Take, for example, the large
Israeli settlement blocs built on land conquered in 1967. The Israelis sought to annex these areas. Yet as the Moratinos Document records, "The Palestinian side stated that blocs would cause
significant harm to the Palestinian interests and rights, particularly to the Palestinians residing in areas Israel seeks to annex."
In particular, the dispute over the Ma'aleh Adumim bloc near
Jerusalem exposed the fundamental difference between the parties on how Security Council Resolution 242—framing the debate
on control of the 1967 territories—should be interpreted. The
Israelis maintain it mandates the withdrawal from "territories"
occupied subsequent to June 4, 1967 while the Palestinians—and
the Arab states whose backing for any accord is critical—insist
that Resolution 242 requires withdrawal from *the* territories, a
return to 1967 with no exceptions. The differing interpretations
produced different results as the Israelis sought to annex nearly
twice as much land as the Palestinians were willing to offer.

5. Akiva Eldar, "Text: 'Moratinos Document'—The Peace that Nearly was at
Taba," *Haaretz*, February 14, 2002. Text of Document dated January 2001 and
available online at www.arts.mcgill.ca/MEPP/PRRN/papers/moratinos.html.

As regards Jerusalem, the parties had agreed in principle to maintain it as an "open city," described by the Moratinos Document as "territory that citizens of both countries can enter without passing through any checkpoints." However, "the Palestinians wanted it to encompass all of Jerusalem, while the Israelis wanted it limited to the Old City only." Considering both parties desire Jerusalem as their respective capital, this constituted a very substantial difference.[6]

The two sides also failed to agree on how much of the Western Wall is sacred to Jews. This dispute speaks to a host of claims by the parties. That is, because the Western Wall is sacred to Jews but occupies the Harem al-Sharif (the Temple Mount) holy to Muslims, Palestinians cannot concede sovereignty over the Temple Mount less they lose the support of the broader Muslim world while Israeli concessions, vis-à-vis the Western Wall, jeopardize the Jewish nature of the state. Debating the extent to which the Western Wall is sacred to Jews thereby raised existential, religious, and territorial issues that would have to be resolved before any agreement could be reached.

On one land issue, however, there seemed no dispute. As the Moratinos Document offers: "Neither side presented any maps over the Gaza Strip. It was implied that the Gaza Strip will be under total Palestinian sovereignty, but details have still to be worked out." Indeed, the principle details discussed involved the question of sovereignty over the land bridge linking Gaza to the West Bank in order that the new Palestinian state be contiguous; there was no debate over control of Gaza per se.

In the years following Taba, Israeli scholars, journalists, and government officials would scan the record for any hint that the two sides had agreed on a framework for resolving the core ques-

6. Ibid.

tion of refugees. What they would find instead was a fairly minor tinkering with the modalities of implementing a settlement but nothing to suggest that Yasser Arafat and his colleagues had budged from their insistence that ultimately those displaced by the 1948 fighting (and their descendents) be permitted to return to Israel. This position was expressed more by the failure of the two sides to embrace the "Clinton Parameters" than by a battle over the modalities of implementation. Under the parameters, the refugees could have been settled inside Israel, within the soon-to-be-created Palestinian state—including land transferred by Israel to that state as part of a "swap" for land annexed by Israel outside its pre-1967 borders—within the country where they were residing when the deal was clinched, or in some other country, with the final say in each case resting with the host government. This was a proposal for settling the issue once and for all, but instead the parties spent much of their time discussing the number of Palestinians who could return to Israel during the first three to five years following the accord. This was an utterly hollow approach, allowing both sides to claim noteworthy advances. Thus, left-wing Israeli negotiator Yossi Bcilin and his colleagues could brag of the great progress made and constructive atmosphere achieved while the Palestinians could maintain that they had betrayed not so much as a word from General Assembly Resolution 194, which Palestinians say accords their refugees the right to return to their pre-1948 homes or villages so long as they agree to live in peace with their neighbors.[7]

A second imperative source on the refugee question comes from documents obtained by the French newspaper *Le Monde* in the late summer of 2001 containing the draft positions of each

7. Ibid. See also David Matz, "Trying to Understand the Taba Talks (Part I)," *Palestine-Israel Journal of Politics, Economics, and Culture* 10, no. 3 (2003): 104.

side.[8] Though formally only "draft positions," these remained the de facto negotiating positions through at least January 2001 as reflected in subsequent drafts and negotiations up through Taba. Though the December 2000 Clinton Parameters provided a coherent plan for settling the refugee issue, the two sides did not significantly alter their positions. Specifically, the Palestinian proposal argued at Taba still provides that "all refugees who wish to return *to their homes* in Israel and live at peace with their neighbors have the right to do so."[9]

The Israeli position, meanwhile, reminded the parties that after accepting all UN resolutions dividing Mandate Palestine into Jewish and Palestinian states, "the emergent state of Israel became embroiled in the war and bloodshed of 1948–49, that led to victims and suffering on both sides, including the displacement and dispossession of the Palestinian civilian population." The Israelis, in other words, would embrace an historical narrative in which they shared *responsibility* for the refugee problem but not one in which they assumed *blame*. Further, they noted that Palestinian aspirations can be satisfied by the establishment of their own sovereign state together with a right of self-determination that includes the ability of a designated capped number to return to Israel. Due to demographic trends, Israel can go no further than that if it seeks to remain a Jewish state. By contrast, the Palestinian insistence on the right of return for refugees is, in effect, a proposal for a two-state solution, but with both of the states Palestinian, one now and one after demography does its work.[10]

---

8. Le Monde Diplomatique's Refugee Papers (2) Israel's "Private response to Palestinian refugee paper of January 22, 2001," Taba, January 23, 2001, Draft 2; (1) Palestinian Refugees Paper, Taba, 22 January 2001 at www.arts.mcgill.ca/mepp/new_prrn/research/research_documents.htm.

9. Ibid.

10. Ibid.

Other participant accounts of the talks have fleshed out the positions described above, none with greater comprehensiveness or authenticity than that of Dennis Ross, Mr. Clinton's Middle East specialist and the man who played the same role for Presidents Ronald Reagan and George H.W. Bush. Ross portrays Yasser Arafat as a man unable or unwilling to close a deal requiring serious compromise. In the period between the Camp David talks of July 2000 and the Taba negotiations mentioned above, for example, Arafat agreed on the need for a demilitarized Palestinian state but never on what the specific limits would be. He embraced territorial compromise but turned down Clinton's plan for delivering 94–96 percent of the West Bank to the Palestinians together with a 3 percent land swap and a nonsovereignty right-of-way linking Gaza and the West Bank. When it came to Jerusalem, he rejected Israeli sovereignty over its own Western Wall. And, in the true moment of truth, he rejected any and all of Clinton's plans for solving the refugee problem.[11]

Coupled with the increasingly violent course of the Second Intifada, the failures at Camp David and Taba are widely assessed as having "discredited" the Israeli peace movement. This is true only in a narrow sense. Ehud Barak, architect of dramatic openings to Syria and the Palestinians, lost his bid for reelection in a rout. Ariel Sharon, the arch hawk, mastermind of Israel's disastrous intervention in Lebanon in the early 1980s, former political pariah, and zealous proponent of settling the 1967 Territories (earning him the sobriquet of the "Bulldozer") was now prime minister. Labor's Knesset mandates fell below two dozen for the first time in Israel's history.

Still, several underlying realities of Israel's situation had not changed; these would soon have more of an impact on Israeli

---

11. See Dennis Ross, *The Missing Peace* (New York: Farrar, Straus, and Co., 2004), pp. 712–58, for specifics on the back-and-forth dialogue.

policy than the "discrediting" of the peace movement. The first was demography. As early as 2001, centrist Likud figures like Dan Meridor and Michael Eitan noted ethnic trends that would eventually make Jews a minority in the land they governed, spurring them to urge serious consideration of proposals to withdraw from areas that were clearly Palestinian. Zionism may have meant settling all the land west of the Jordan, encompassing Israel, the West Bank, and the Gaza Strip. But it also meant establishing a state populated mainly, if not exclusively, by Jews. As of the 2000 census, Jews numbered only 51 percent of the population in this region. Palestinian Arabs, non-Jewish Russians, Druze and foreign workers accounted for the rest. Their higher birthrates meant that within a few years, Jews would be a minority in their own country plus the land they occupied, and would either have to invoke increasingly repressive measures to maintain political control, or surrender that control in the name of democracy. During an interview at his wood-paneled Tel Aviv skyscraper office, former prime minister Barak defined the issue succinctly:

> Between the Jordan River and the Mediterranean there live eleven million people, four and a half million Palestinians and six and a half million Israelis. If there is only one political entity ruling over there named Israel, it will become inevitably either non-Jewish or non-democratic. Inevitably! Neither option is good. So there is a compelling advantage to separate, to disengage.[12]

The issue can, however, be overstated. With this analysis, a key question became: what percentage of the included population could you occupy and oppress and still maintain both your Jewish and democratic credentials. Forty-nine percent? Thirty percent? Twenty percent . . . the current non-Jewish Israeli citizen popu-

---

12. Ehud Barak, transcript of interview with author, Tel Aviv, August 17, 2005.

lation inside the Green Line demarking the pre-1967 borders? There was no silver bullet without going all the way back to those 1967 borders. But clearly the "Greater Israel" approach could only aggravate the demographic issue.

A second factor was security. During the 2001–2002 period, the Palestinians increasingly resorted to suicide attacks inside Israel. Busses, restaurants, cafes, market places, and a discothèque all became targets, killing hundreds, maiming thousands, and choking tourism. Such attacks turned the most mundane of life's activities into perilous adventures for a people increasingly fearful of losing their national sanity but also wary of encouraging the terrorists should they depart from their ordinary pursuits. Yet to a visitor during the 2002 period of most savage attack, Israel maintained an air of defiant normalcy, with roads clogged, busses packed and markets, cafes, and restaurants well attended.

Even this collective courage proved insufficient. Things threatened to get worse as the Palestinians attempted to stage a mega-incident on the scale of 9/11. One foiled plot involved using a car bomb in the parking lot to collapse one of the Azrieli Towers, the tallest skyscrapers in downtown Tel Aviv.[13] In another incident, the putative suicide driver of a truck filled with explosive material tried to ignite a natural gas tank farm at Pi Glilot, just south of Herzliya.[14] Only one small blaze resulted and the fire was quickly extinguished. Yet although no incidents akin to September 11 succeeded, the attempts were sufficient in and of themselves, increasing the siege mentality of the Israeli populace and raising the specter of inevitable and prolonged violence.[15]

13. Jerusalem Post Staff, "IDF Thwarts Bid to Bomb Azrieli Towers," *Jerusalem Post*, April 29, 2002.

14. David Rudge, "Pi Glilot Attack Raises Questions," *Jerusalem Post*, May 24, 2002.

15. David Rudge, "Ben-Eliezer Warns of Bombing Wave. Catastrophe Averted at Pi Glilot," *Jerusalem Post*, May 24, 2002.

By far the most significant political change was less the discrediting of peace advocates than the discrediting of the Palestinians as negotiating partners. Despite lip service to a so-called "two state solution" to the long-running dispute, Israelis were increasingly convinced that the real objective of Yasser Arafat and his colleagues was the destruction of the Jewish state through terrorism, demographics, or some combination of the two. That alone could explain the continuing insistence on the right of return, the systematic support to terrorism, the honors paid the Palestinian "martyrs," the direct involvement of groups like the al-Aqsa Martyrs Brigade—an offshoot of Arafat's own Fatah movement—in the violence, and Arafat's attempt to up the ante by importing fifty tons of advanced weapons from Iran aboard the intercepted cargo ship Karyn A.

Professor Dan Schueftan of Haifa University, a combative scholar with a searing wit, was among the first of the Israeli intellectuals to argue that the demographic challenge posed by the Palestinians is no less severe than the security threat, that there is no foreseeable negotiating option and that the situation presents Israel with the need to disengage unilaterally from the Gaza Strip and those parts of the West Bank that are either too remote to defend efficiently or too close to existing Palestinian communities. During an interview in his Ramat Aviv duplex apartment, he argued that negotiations with the Palestinians were an exercise in futility:

> Even those Palestinians who are saying we are willing to accept
> for the moment a state on the West Bank and the Gaza Strip
> are still saying, but we need Israel to recognize the profound
> injustice that Israel caused us in 1948, and therefore the 1948
> issue is not closed, and you have at least to admit your guilt—
> which will be an everlasting guilt—and you must start a process
> that would allow Palestinians in large numbers to come into

Israel, change the demographic balance, and in the final analysis this will not be a Jewish state.

"We live in a bad neighborhood, and when you live in a bad neighborhood, being nice doesn't cut it," Schueftan continued. "In order for Israel to survive, it has to cut itself off completely from Palestinians. And the danger of a Palestinian terrorist is not as big as the danger of a Palestinian migrant into Israel who changes the demographic composition of the state of Israel."[16]

The notion of adding some sort of physical barrier on the West Bank to offer protection from terrorist infiltration and delineate the border of the Israeli state was soon added to the dual-idea of unilateral Israeli withdrawal and Israeli-Palestinian separation. Credit for integrating the two ideas is disputed, but western diplomats paid to know such things insist the parentage belongs to Eival Giladi, at the time head of strategic planning for the IDF. They say Giladi had floated the idea in several private conversations and authored a secret memo on the subject late in 2001 or early the following year. During the course of a March 3, 2006, News Hour interview with the BBC, Giladi recalled the pitch he had made directly to Sharon: "I came to Prime Minister Sharon and asked him very simply, you know we enjoy military superiority, we are so stronger politically. Why do we have to let the extremists of the other side shape the future of everyone here? Why can't we take action which must be balanced?"

Amos Malka, head of the IDF's Intelligence Branch, was quick to sign on; so was Avi Dichter, head of Shin Bet. An Israeli military planner present at several relevant meetings insists that Dichter soon became the most zealous advocate of the fence. "It became like a mantra with Dichter," he recalled. "He raised it every time we talked about stopping the suicide bombers." Even

16. Dan Schueftan, transcript of interview with author, Tel Aviv, August 1, 2005.

with Sharon having reoccupied parts of the West Bank ceded by
Oslo for Palestinian administration, the strategists saw a deteri-
orating situation with nothing in sight save continuing terrorist
penetrations. During an early morning interview at Tel Aviv's Jaffee Center for Strategic Studies, Dichter claimed that without a
fence, suicide attacks could not be stopped:

> There is nothing between the terror centers and the living cen-
> ters in Israel. To cross from Nablus to Tel Aviv is easier than to
> cross from New Jersey to New York—at least there you have a
> river. So we convinced people to build the fence—that we
> needed the physical buffer zone. We also convinced them that
> fighting from the outside with no fence would lead us no-
> where.[17]

Barak, a defeated politician but still a defense intellectual to
be reckoned with, likewise embraced the idea of a fence. So did
the Likud MKs Eitan and Meridor. Independently, they briefed
Sharon on the idea but did not specifically address the questions
of precisely where the fence would go or what would be done to
the settlements in the West Bank lying beyond it. Sharon, who
could at times convey all the conviction of a sphinx, gave no
indication of either interest or noninterest. Nor was there any
political pressure for him to act. His Laborite defense minister,
Binyamin Ben-Eliezer, was against the proposal, fearing it would
bring about a repetition of the pullout from Lebanon which was
proclaimed by Hezbollah as proof that Israel could succumb to
sustained military pressure, a lesson the Palestinians took to
heart. No, argued Ben-Eliezer, unilateral Israeli separation "would
be seen as a reward for terror and invite more terror."[18]

Neither was the United States enthralled with the move. In

17. Avi Dicther, author's notes of interview, Tel Aviv, August 1, 2005.
18. Susser, "Fence."

his farewell address, departing U.S. ambassador Martin Indyk told a Tel Aviv University audience: "Because it will not be recognized, because it will remain controversial, because you will retain some territories beyond the June 4, 1967 lines, the last line of your withdrawal will become the first line of Palestinian attack. If you think mortars are a problem now, imagine what it could become then."[19]

Indyk left Israel in July 2001. Over the next several months, Labor and others on the left became increasingly infatuated with the idea of a unilateral separation coupled with a wall or fence that followed the 1967 boundaries, perhaps encompassing the settlement blocs as well. Some agreed with Meridor that the Israeli move could induce the Palestinians to return to the negotiating table, but most did not regard this as a paramount objective or its potential failure as a defect of the strategy. Nor did Indyk's fear of a hostile Palestinian state committed to regaining territory outside the 1967 borders Israel might try to hold bother too many on the left. After all, Israel had been surrounded by hostile neighbors from its creation through the peace with Egypt and had managed to survive. Up to and including the Six Days' War, it had held the moral high ground, fighting only in self-defense, governing only those Arabs who resided inside its own boundaries, imposing a colonial-style regime on no one. Many on the left had opposed settlements from the start. They warned that settling on the land of others would undermine the Israeli character and lead to a form of exploitation that would cost Israel support throughout the democratic West. Over subsequent decades, they watched "creeping annexation," with disgust as settlers murdered Palestinian mayors and committed countless acts of violence and intimidation against the Palestinian residents while the state looked

19. Ibid.

the other way and the number of settlers grew from fifty thousand
to a hundred thousand to the current two hundred and forty
thousand. Perhaps most distressing was that Labor began the settlement policy and, during its brief periods of power after the
mid-1970s, did little to rein it in, even after Oslo. Now they argued, it was time to disengage. The absence of a Palestinian negotiating partner should not determine the character of Israel.
With the help of a physical barrier to counter the new threat of
the suicide bomber, Israel could both defend and define itself.

Sharon read the signals. Those who have watched him over
the years comment that Sharon was far more of a consensus
builder than many critics realize, but also very much more a tactician than a strategist. His Lebanon debacle of the early 1980s
had convinced him that big moves require both Labor support
and acquiescence by the United States. Unilateral disengagement
was a concept he was not nearly ready to embrace in 2001–2002.
Not only was it a coalition killer in terms of alienating his right-
wing coalition partners, but much of his own party would likely
bolt at the idea.

If disengagement was a nonstarter at the time, the construction of a wall separating the two populaces was a middle-of-the-
road approach that would placate Labor. There were, however,
drawbacks to this avenue as well. Sharon himself had expressed
doubts about the project, concerned that it might be interpreted
as an Israeli statement of sovereignty over the fenced area, more
a border than a buffer, a move he was similarly not ready to make
at this time. Also, military and intelligence views on the subject
were by no means unanimous. Dichter, Malka, and Giladi aside,
others like IDF chief-of-staff Moshe Ya'Alon saw the fence as a
prelude to unilateral disengagement, which he warned would be
interpreted as an Israeli military defeat. Other IDF officials argued
that close to 55 percent of the suicide bombers entered Israel
through ruse and disguise at legal checkpoints. A wall—we

should use the term *separation barrier* rather than wall, as only 5 percent of the barrier is wall—could not impede such infiltration, while making an elaborate search of all vehicles traveling to and from West Bank destinations each day would choke ordinary commerce beyond endurance.

Still, Sharon finally agreed to the fence in the summer of 2002, purporting to sever it from the concept of unilateral disengagement. This was an illusion. Irrespective of adjustments in the route designed to bring additional settlements within its protection, a majority of settlements and at least fifty-eight thousand of the two hundred and forty thousand Israelis living on the West Bank would fall outside its perimeters. Yes, Israeli troops could range where they wanted. Checkpoints and searches would offer some protection. But the fence would come to define the 8 percent of the West Bank Israel was committed to protecting, and also the land it would be willing to give up, just as the fence built in Gaza in the mid-1990s had separated land many could not wait to get rid of from Israel's beloved Negev.

Sharon, a man defined by actions and rarely by words, remained cryptic, describing the fence as "only another counterterrorism measure." He denied unilateral separation was even under consideration. During the political campaign that fall and winter, Labor candidate Amram Mitzna proposed a substantial unilateral withdrawal from Gaza if negotiations proved impossible. Sharon famously replied, "The fate of Netzarim is the fate of Tel Aviv."[20] He and Likud overwhelmingly won the January 2003 election, taking forty-one seats in the one-hundred-and-twenty-member Knesset to only nineteen for Labor, and formed a right-wing coalition that excluded Labor. Along the way, Sharon cemented ties with the Bush administration which, due largely to 9/11 and the

20. Peter Hirschberg, "Background/Sharon Talks Regional Peace to American Jews," *Haaretz*, April 24, 2002.

resulting War on Terror, had come a long way from its periodic scolding of Sharon for military thrusts taken in response to terrorist incidents.

That did not happen overnight. After the World Trade Center destruction, Washington gave Arafat an opportunity to pull the plug on the Second Intifada. On April 4, 2002, as Israeli forces responded to the Passover bombing with incursions deep into Palestinian territory, President Bush urged Israel to pull back, embraced the recent call of peace broker George Mitchell for an end to both terrorism and new Israeli settlement activity, and articulated his vision of a just settlement as "two states, Israel and Palestine, living side by side in peace and security."[21]

But as Arafat again shunned an opening for productive talks and was forced by Israeli military power to take refuge in the Muqata, his administrative complex in Ramallah, the president delivered a message on June 24, 2002 with an entirely different tone:

> Peace requires a new and different Palestinian leadership so that a Palestinian state can be born. I call on the Palestinian people to elect leaders, leaders not compromised by terrorism [. . .] And the United States will not support the establishment of a Palestinian State until its leaders engage in a sustained fight against terrorism and dismantle its infrastructure.[22]

Sharon could reasonably conclude that the president had given him a period of grace in which to focus on combating the terrorist campaign against Israel's very existence. In such an environment major political initiatives could be shunned while security measures took precedence. Arafat—under pressure from Egypt's Hosni Mubarak and much of the international commu-

21. President George W. Bush, the Rose Garden, "President to Send Secretary Powell to Middle East," April 4, 2002, 11:00 a.m. EST.
22. President George W. Bush, the Rose Garden, "President Bush Calls for New Palestinian Leadership," June 24, 2002, 3:47 P.M.

nity—seemed finally to grasp the message, naming Mahmoud Abbas (Abu Mazen) prime minister. Abbas, a longtime Arafat colleague and one of his fellow "Tunisians," was regarded by the Israelis as a promising personality, assuming Arafat gave him room to breathe. True, he had authored a book suggesting the number of Jews killed in the Holocaust was closer to one million than six million; true, he lacked a political base of his own. And, like many of the insiders he had made a fortune during the Oslo period, residing in a four-story multimillion dollar Gaza villa that was probably not built with the proceeds of soccer bets, so he could be vulnerable to an anticorruption campaign. But very early on—even before it became a suicide bombing campaign—he had expressed opposition to the Second Intifada, arguing that violence at that point was harmful to the Palestinian cause. Furthermore, he seemed to recognize the need to streamline and control the security forces, which to that point had been organized by Arafat in a fashion that both minimized the threat any single armed faction could pose to the PA leadership and made it next to impossible to control any maverick unit from doing what it pleased.

As Sharon turned to combating terrorism in the newly reoccupied areas, the proposals for unilateral separation had been reduced in terms of policy to construction of a wall and little else.

3. Sharon's Surprise

ON DECEMBER 18, 2003, in an address to the fourth Herzliya Conference on Israeli National Security, Ariel Sharon stunned his own nation, the Palestinians, and much of the rest of the world by embracing the concept of unilateral disengagement in a way that would mean the dismemberment of an unspecified number of existing settlements. First he would seek talks with the Palestinians under the so-called Road Map formula articulated by the Bush administration the previous April 30. But if the Palestinians would not or could not join the process, "then Israel will initiate the unilateral security step of disengagement from the Palestinians."[1] Specifically, the plan would involve "the redeployment of IDF forces along new security lines and a change in the deployment of settlements, which will reduce as much as possible the number of Israelis located in the heart of the Palestinian population."[2]

To repeat: "This reduction of friction will require the extremely difficult step of changing the deployment of some of the settlements."[3] In an early February interview with the pro-pullout newspaper *Haaretz*, Sharon identified the twenty-one Gaza and four Samaria settlements targeted for dismemberment. These were intended as security measures, not an attempt to redefine

1. Address by PM Ariel Sharon at the Fourth Herzliya Conference, December 18, 2003.
2. Ibid.
3. Ibid.

Israel's borders. To underline the defensive nature of the move, work on the fence would be accelerated.[4]

The attempt to interpret Sharon's action engaged journalists, diplomats, and members of the national security and political communities as had few other decisions in the nation's history. To a large extent, this was due to the importance of the decision itself, which was widely assessed as a 180-degree turn on an issue of fundamental importance to Israel's future. But without the irony of the move, much of the electricity in the debate would have been absent. After all, this was the Bulldozer at work, the former young commando who had led raids into Arab villages not always free of the taint of excess. Here was the Suez-crossing hero of the 1973 war. Here was a man who was taking a step nearly certain to split the Likud Party he helped form by aligning his miserable splinter party Shlomzion with the far larger Liberal Party and Menachem Begin's Herut. Here was a defense minister who had deceived his country into a maximalist Lebanon campaign that ended with a humiliating pullback and included mass murders committed by Sharon's Falangist allies at two Palestinian refugee camps for which an Israeli tribunal concluded he bore "indirect responsibility." Here was a cabinet minister who urged Israelis to construct a settlement on every hilltop and who as prime minister allowed fifty-two illegal settlement outposts to get started, barely lifting a finger to shut down more than a handful of them.

Simple enough, explained his admirers. In his old age—he was seventy-five in 2003—Sharon was searching for a legacy. If Greater Israel was not to be had, then an Israel with realistic borders, demographically cohesive and secure living side by side with a nonthreatening Palestinian state was the next-best alternative. In the end a treaty would be required following bilateral talks. But the time was not at hand and so Israel had to act alone.

4. "Disengagement Timeline," *Haaretz Special Magazine*, August 15, 2005.

A number of factors combined to convince Sharon that the time was ripe to act. The first was the quick collapse of the Abu Mazen prime ministerial gambit. President Bush brokered a June 4, 2003, meeting in Aqaba, Jordan involving himself, King Abdullah, Hosni Mubarak, Abu Mazen, and Sharon. The president hoped the chemistry between Sharon and Abu Mazen would be good. Whether or not it was, Sharon delivered very little of what Abu Mazen needed to enhance his political standing back home: prisoners released, checkpoints reduced, travel restrictions eased, curfews ended, the Israeli presence cut sharply. Simply put, with the Second Intifada still pulsing, Sharon had little to offer in any of these areas. And when Abu Mazen returned to Ramallah, he found Arafat working busily to eliminate any of the prime minister's control over security matters. Without Arafat's backing, his ability to control groups like Hamas, Palestinian Islamic Jihad (PIJ), or Fatah's own al-Aqsa Martyrs Brigades was nonexistent. By early September, Abu Mazen had resigned; his successor, Ahmed Qureia (Abu Ala), was not a man Sharon trusted.

Second was Sharon's hesitancy about immediately getting involved in Road Map negotiations despite his conditional endorsement of the approach. Presented by President Bush in the heady aftermath of the American military charge to Baghdad, the plan had three essential phases. The first places heavy burdens on the Palestinian side in terms of reforming their political structure and security apparatus and, most important, dismantling the infrastructure of terrorism. The Road Map describes that obligation in these words: "Palestinians declare an unequivocal end to violence and terrorism and undertake visible efforts on the ground to arrest, disrupt and restrain individuals and groups conducting and planning violent attacks on Israelis anywhere."[5]

5. BBC, "The Roadmap: Full Text," *BBC News*, 30 April, 2003, 17:11 GMT. Available online at http://news.bbc.co.uk/2/hi/middle_east/2989783.stm.

By contrast, Israel's chief obligations in phase one are fairly modest: dismantle illegal outposts, quit expanding settlements, and withdraw to the pre-Intifada lines of September 28, 2000. If strictly enforced, the period could be critical as it puts the principal Israeli concern—security—ahead of everything else. Sharon would later regard the Road Map as an asset. At first, however, he had little confidence that the "Quartet" of parties involved with the initiative—the United States, the United Nations, the European Union, and Russia—would, with the exception of the United States, demand very much from the Palestinians and so Israel's incentive to actively assist the Palestinians in their obligations was minimal.

Sharon liked the optional phase two better as it suggests the establishment of a Palestinian state, possibly with provisional borders, while such final status issues as permanent borders, refugees, Jerusalem, and security are negotiated. These things could take a while, a very long while, to resolve despite the Road Map's ambitious three-year implementation scheme. A senior western diplomat confessed: "I don't know what, if anything, Sharon's intention is regarding a Palestinian state. His approach is a very long-term slowly evolving arrangement that ends in a shape nobody sees now."[6] What Sharon saw as the strength of phase two, the Palestinians regarded as a possible means of trapping them permanently inside provisional borders; they have from the outset urged all parties to leapfrog over phase two.

In dozens of unofficial conversations with westerners and potentially sympathetic Israelis, the Palestinians were from the start pleading forbearance. Whether cooped up in the Moqata or set free to mobilize support for the Israeli initiative, Yasser Arafat could not immediately bring the terrorists to heel. Yet neither could anyone else. The major terrorist movement—Hamas—and splinter factions such as the Palestinian Islamic Jihad, could only

6. Interview with senior western diplomat, July 22, 2005.

be co-opted by the prospect of statehood. A move to physically disarm them could provoke civil war. Phase two, with the option of provisional borders would encourage mischief. Israel would go about its typical business of creating facts on the ground during the provisional period, leaving the Palestinians at a severe disadvantage in the final status talks. Why not move directly to the phase three period and settle the dispute once and for all?

To security-conscious Israelis, this was a totally unacceptable plan. They could easily envision the United Nations, the European Union, and the Russians lining up behind the Palestinians on one issue after another, with the United States winding up as an honest broker trying to nudge the Israelis along. That was to be avoided at all costs.

The Road Map was not the only formula bothering Sharon. In October 2003, a group of leftist Israeli reserve officers, members of the Knesset, and peace advocates, working with a somewhat less illustrious Palestinian contingent, released a "Virtual Peace Accord," signed in Geneva following lengthy negotiations. Leading the Israeli side was former justice minister and Taba negotiator Yossi Beilin, a man whose empathy for the Palestinian predicament had reached the point where the very mention of his name invited quips and ridicule among more defense-minded Israelis. "Yossi Beilin is a very, very sophisticated political manipulator," snapped Dan Schueftan during one discussion on the Geneva Virtual Accord. "I wish we had somebody like him on the Israeli side."[7]

On the Palestinian side, former PA minister of culture and information, Yasser Abed Rabbo, led the Palestinian team. The juxtaposition of a justice minister versus a press spokesman was not lost on Israelis, many of whom felt the Israeli team was seeking to make policy while the Palestinians sought propaganda

---

7. Dan Schueftan, transcript of interview with author, Tel Aviv, August 1, 2005.

points. The deal itself, meanwhile, did not explicitly permit Israel to annex its major settlement blocs, instead permitting both sides to swap land on a 1:1 basis, each beginning with the 1967 borders. By contrast, the Clinton Parameters implicitly gave Israel the settlement blocs while leaving the Palestinians with 94–96 percent of their prewar holdings plus a 3 percent "land swap." The Palestinians also increased their hold on a divided Jerusalem under Virtual Geneva. Most critically, under a vague and confusing refugee formula, the Palestinians could well have argued that the Israelis obligated themselves to repatriate as many refugees as the average of individual Arab countries—including Palestine itself—had committed themselves to accept. Admittedly, there were other, more limited interpretations of Israeli responsibility for refugees, but the document lends itself to expansive interpretation. A senior western diplomat offered this sketch of Geneva: "According to Geneva, Israel loses a lot of settlements, gets a lot of Palestinians, and Jerusalem is divided."[8]

Sharon's concern about Geneva was compounded when Secretary of State Colin Powell invited leading members of the negotiating teams to Washington to receive his benediction, an event Powell managed without embracing the specific terms of the deal. Nonetheless, to Jerusalem the inference was clear: move unilaterally and you retain substantial control over events; play the waiting game and you may wind up with the United States pressing you to accept the Road Map process and the Virtual Geneva terms. Sharon, the consummate tactician, would not let that happen. As his senior advisor, Dov Weissglass, would later brag, withdrawing from Gaza was one way to put the Road Map "in formaldehyde."[9]

Demographics undoubtedly played the decisive role in the

8. Interview with senior western diplomat, July 22, 2005.
9. Ari Shavit, "The Big Freeze," *Haaretz Magazine*, October 8, 2004.

prime minister's evolution on unilateralism. A military planner participating in several meetings with Sharon during the 2002–2004 period recalls him as being exceptionally attentive whenever the subject of population projections arose. Another factor was the cost of protecting the settlements. Sharon was becoming convinced that except for military activity related to protecting Gaza settlers, Israelis were giving up very little by pulling out. As Avi Dichter noted, "We have had the fence there since '95. In the last five years we haven't had one suicide bomber who succeeded in crossing the fence."[10] Now and then the Israelis would launch a targeted assassination inside Gaza. The IDF would also come to the rescue of settlements under attack, or retaliate when they had been too late for the rescue. In the main, though, the place was left for Palestinians to run even before the pullout.

Perhaps the most authoritative account of the government's metamorphosis on the issue is offered by Ehud Olmert, the gravel-voiced Cuban cigar-puffing bundle of energy who previously served ten years as mayor of Jerusalem, beginning with an upset victory over the iconic Teddy Kollek and continuing with two successful bids for reelection. He finally resigned, responding to Sharon's invitation to join his government, the Knesset having passed a law forbidding sitting mayors from serving in that body.[11] Once in national government, Olmert became Sharon's most loyal ally, his political alter ego. By the time withdrawal began, he was serving as Sharon's deputy prime minister as well as his finance minister (the post Binyamin Netanyahu vacated over disagreement with the pullout), his minister of industry,

10. Avi Dicther, notes of interview with author, Tel Aviv, August 1, 2005. Now a senior member of the Kadima Knesset delegation, Dichter's views on such matters as future West Bank withdrawals and security arrangements are influential if not decisive.

11. Ehud Olmert, transcript of interview with author, Jerusalem, August 19, 2005.

trade and labor, and the head of the Israel Lands administration. When Sharon suffered an incapacitating stroke on January 4, 2006, Olmert became acting prime minister. Later, he was nominated to head the Kadima (Forward) Party founded by Sharon just weeks before his stroke, winning enough seats to form the new government.

Like Sharon, Olmert traveled a long and tortuous path to Gush Katif. The son of a prominent Herut Party family, Olmert grew up in the right-wing Betar youth movement. Too young to have been among the founders of the state and with only a modest war record, Olmert differed from each of the country's former prime ministers, instead joining the likes of Dan Meridor and Beni Begin as "Princes," or, in the case of Tsipi Livni, a princess of the Likud. He was still far to the right when, as a young Kenesset member in 1978, he watched with disgust as Anwar Sadat and Menachem Begin concluded their historic "land for peace" accord. Olmert voted against the treaty, saying Israel should hold onto all the land it had conquered in the 1967 war. Only after it became clear to him that Zionism would never draw enough Jews into the Greater Israel area to match Palestinian numbers on the West Bank and Gaza did his position evolve to one of unilateral disengagement. After his appointment to replace Netanyahu, Olmert acknowledged his early error, saying "I voted against Menachem Begin, I told him it was a historic mistake, how dangerous it would be, and so on, and so on. Now I am sorry he is not alive for me to be able to publicly recognize his wisdom and my mistake. He was right and I was wrong. Thank God we pulled out of the Sinai."[12]

Olmert's claims his conversion was pragmatic. Unable to win an open-ended demographic battle with the Palestinians, the Israeli state had to fashion its own solution to maintain its Jewish nature. He saw no benefit to talks with the Palestinian leadership,

12. Ibid.

his view of it conditioned by the bloody aftermaths of shootings and suicide bombings he had inspected as mayor of Jerusalem, by Arafat punctuating his protestations of peace with a call for a million *shadids* (martyrs) to march on Jerusalem. "Yasser Arafat," said Olmert, speaking the name in a hollow tone. "It's time that civilized people stop being misled by this treacherous murderer and terrorist who has become the role model for terrorist acts across the world in his repeated brutal attacks on innocent people." Still, he sounded less pragmatic and more defeatist when he told a peace group in the summer of 2005 that, "we are tired of fighting, we are tired of being courageous, we are tired of winning, we are tired of defeating our enemies."[13]

During the course of a shirt-sleeved Friday morning session in his cabinet office, Olmert said he never wanted Jews to rule Palestinians. As a young legislator, he was influenced by Moshe Dayan's call for Palestinian autonomy in the Occupied Territories, allowing the Palestinians themselves to define the contours of what would evolve, Dayan believed, into an independent Palestinian state. Israel had committed itself to Palestinian autonomy in the Camp David Accord with Egypt's Anwar Sadat, but Prime Minister Menachem Begin was far more intent on fortifying future Israeli claims to "Judea" and "Samaria" by building settlements there than he was to implementing the agreement. Accordingly, Begin put Joseph Burg, a National Religious Party foe of autonomy, in charge of that program. Dayan continued to urge pulling back unilaterally, leaving the Palestinians to govern themselves, a formula he felt would produce a natural definition of the border. Frustrated, he finally resigned from the government, leaving Olmert to ponder how to take better advantage of some future opportunity should one be presented.[14]

---

13. Yossi Klein Halevi, "Past Perfect: How Sharon's Successor Could Succeed," *New Republic*, January 23, 2006.
    14. Interview with Olmert.

Olmert maintained that hints of Sharon's emerging views surfaced during the 2001 election campaign when he spoke of the need for "painful sacrifices." According to Olmert, "this is a code. Painful means that it would include pulling out from territories which are more sensitive in the collective memory of the Jewish people." A bit of a stretch? Perhaps, but Olmert had more evidence to offer, "And then he said, already going back to the beginning of 2000, that he will recognize a Palestinian state living alongside the state of Israel. Where would the Palestinian state be? So the most inevitable conclusion would be that, yes, even if Sharon didn't spell it out in so many words, he meant dismantling settlements."[15]

For the first part of his administration, Sharon would retreat when queried about any unilateral Israeli move to defuse the Israeli-Palestinian confrontation; it would be November 2003 before the policy seemed to be evolving, now in a public, now in a private fashion. At the time, the Intifada was still inflicting pain and misery on Israel and Sharon's standing in the polls had slipped to the mid-thirties. In mid-November, Sharon and Weisglass traveled to Rome to meet with Italian president Silvio Berlusconi. As *Haaretz* would later report, it was there, on the night of November 17, that the two Israelis gathered with Elliott Abrams, the top Middle East man on the Bush National Security Council. Notably, Abrams had apparently come to the meeting prepared to discuss an initiative proposed by Syria's president Bashar Asad, in which Sharon had little interest. Instead the two told Abrams that Sharon might shortly be announcing plans to unilaterally evacuate Israeli settlements in Gaza. At the time Sharon was contemplating a partial Gaza withdrawal.

The news was not well received by the Americans, who had hoped to get the Road Map process jump-started and preferred

15. Ibid.

bi-lateral to unilateral arrangements.[16] Eventually the positions of both parties would evolve. The United States would come to accept a unilateral Israeli pullback from Gaza and insist on a modest symbolic withdrawal from the West Bank. Sharon and Olmert, meanwhile, would have preferred an even more ambitious West Bank move. And when he did quit Gaza, Sharon also gave up control over the Philadelphia Corridor separating Egypt from Gaza, a favorite route—both above and below ground—for terrorists and weapons smugglers.

Returning to Israel, Sharon raised the prospect of unilateral action in a talk to the Prime Minister's Business Conference in Tel Aviv, later jibing Olmert, "Ehud, I didn't see that you jumped off your seat when I said unilateral actions." Olmert replied, "I listened very carefully."[17] Carefully enough so that a few weeks later, when Sharon asked him to pinch hit at the annual memorial tribute to David Ben Gurion, "I decided on the spot that I am going to give it a push. And on the grave I made a very, very strong statement about giving up the dream of Greater Israel, which, coming from the vice prime minister and senior Likud spokesman, and so on and so forth, was a very dramatic statement." Shimon Peres hugged him, saying, "This is very dramatic" and Ehud Barak told him the moment was "a historic turning point." Determined to seize the moment and bring his boss along, Olmert followed with an interview in *Yediot Achronnot*, the nation's largest daily, urging a unilateral Israeli pullout from much of Gaza and the West Bank.[18]

His comments provoked a front-page headline story. As Olmert later recounted: "Sharon called me on that day, and he said, 'Are you still in Jerusalem?' And I said, 'Yes.' And he said, 'Is

16. Aluf Benn, "Metamorphosis of Ariel Sharon," *Haaretz Special Magazine*, August 15, 2005.

17. Interview with Olmert.

18. Ibid.

Jerusalem still in our hands after your interview?' And we were laughing and he said, 'I think it's about time that we take a serious step.'"[19]

As the decision to withdraw was being discussed, Olmert combined a caveat for Sharon's course of action with a proposal to go well beyond anything then under consideration:

> I told him, "You have to get ready for a dramatic political change, because the Likud will not survive this." And I said, "Let's start from the beginning on a much bigger, much greater scale operation than just Gaza, because the political devastation will be the same anyway, and you don't want to go in stages— go through this pain every two years—so let's do at the beginning something much bigger that will give us rest for ten or fifteen years."[20]

Sharon thereby agreed to a parallel pullback on the West Bank that included several settlements beyond the four—Ganim, Kadim, Sa-Nur, and Homesh, with their combined ninety-five families—eventually evacuated. Yet then the Americans said, "Don't push too much." The question thereby becomes: who on the administration's team was reticent about going further?

"All of them," Olmert recalled:

> Hadley, Elliot, Condi—mostly Condi, but all of them. I think that the reason is that the American administration wanted that the first phase of disengagement will be a trigger for eventual serious negotiations with the Palestinians and therefore, they didn't want it to be such that, you know, from Israel's point of view would justify parking for many years. So they wanted it to be something, but they wanted it not to be too big from Israel's point of view saying, "Now we have done our share, we want to rest for a few years."[21]

Clearly, as Olmert's narrative suggests, the U.S. administration

19. Ibid.
20. Ibid.
21. Ibid.

wanted enough West Bank settlements evacuated to establish a precedent, but not so many as to compromise the big Gaza initiative or to provide Israel with an excuse to do nothing else on the West Bank for an extended period.

Olmert described the eventual withdrawal as more significant than even the peace agreements with Egypt and Jordan that led to the normalization of diplomatic relations with those two states. That is, "for the first time in the history of the Zionist movement, the Jewish people decided to turn the tide and to make a U-turn, if you will, in the most sensitive point in the Zionist ethos, which is settlements."[22] The chance is presently at hand, in other words, to secure a dramatic redefinition of the Israeli enterprise concomitantly with a change in the political status quo.

Sharon faced some tricky political business following disclosure of his pullout plans. Senior political advisers urged him to seek a national referendum on the pullout, but Sharon demurred, allowing his right-wing erstwhile allies to seize the moment. Thirteen members of his own party, led by the consistent if not charismatic Uzi Landau, withdrew their support for his government alongside a smattering of right-wing Knesset members. He immediately set about replacing the departed votes by inviting Labor and its nineteen Knesset votes into the coalition, but it was not until the autumn of 2004 that he won formal approval from his party, Likud, to make the deal. Earlier his own central committee rebelled, voting first to reject the planned withdrawals and later to demand a referendum on the question. The former action followed perhaps the most successful political move by the Yesha Council of its entire campaign, thousands of council members going door to door to rally Central Committee members to the task.

Not all of the opposition to the pullout was emotional and religious. A number of respected military strategists also stepped forward to challenge the security ramifications of Sharon's move.

22. Ibid.

None were more effective than Yaakov Amidror, a hard-line re-
tired major general. Writing in the December 2004 issue of the
Jaffee Center for Strategic Studies' *Strategic Assessment*, Amidror
called the move, "a strategic error of historical magnitude." In the
first place, the withdrawal would feed the Palestinian myth that
terrorism defeated Israel. The result would be that Qassam rockets would target Ashkelon, Sderot, and other Negev towns in an
expanded series of attacks and the influence of terrorist organizations would grow. "Thus, Israel is about to establish a state in
Gaza, a state in which Hamas will have freedom of action and be
joined by the umbilical cord to Hizbollah." The contagion could
thereupon spread to the West Bank where Israel had been waging
a successful anti-terrorist campaign to that point. Amidror also
expressed concern that the IDF and Shin Bet would lose assets
on the ground that would become less vulnerable to Israeli control. "At the heart of terrorist infrastructures are the leaders, the
commanders in the field, the operatives, the laboratories, and
they can be attacked."[23]

But maybe not after the withdrawal. Maybe then the threat
from the West Bank will point directly at the heart of Israel's
major cities. "The Palestinian strategy will be clear: the creation
of a threat against Israel's home front, while waging a terrorist
and guerrilla war under the protection of their umbrella that prevents Israel from retaliation."[24] From what was perhaps the
world's most successful anti-terrorism campaign, Israel was reaching out to embrace unnecessary defeat.

Opposition to the withdrawal, however, suffered from five
factors that increasingly made Sharon look more and more like a
winner. The first was an inability by opponents to make a fundamental decision on what they were all about. Were they reli-

23. Yaakov Amidror, "The Unilateral Withdrawal: A Security Error of
Historical Magnitude," *Strategic Assessment* 7, no. 3 (December 2004).
    24. Ibid.

gious or secular? Should their opposition be active or passive? Were they battling for victory here and now, or building a constituency for big battles to come later on the West Bank?

Paradoxically, the answer might well have been all of the above. At times the foes of withdrawal slashed tires and blocked busy roads and streets. Then they wore orange and handed out ribbons. Some rabbis urged soldiers to ignore their commanders and refuse to evict settlers while others simply urged commanders to consider the moral qualms of their troops when assigning tasks. Two rabbis issued a *pulsa denura*, pleading with God's angels to strike Sharon dead, a black plea that recalled a similar injunction with Yitzhak Rabin as the target.[25] One can only imagine their mystical joy upon receiving word of Sharon's brain hemorrhage.

At the end, most settlers and their allies accepted their fate with little more than passive resistance. Simply put, the militant settlers may not have had an option given the vast capabilities of the IDF and other security forces. The evacuation of the Maoz Yam hotel at Gush Katif had been accomplished in less time than it would take to watch one quarter of a basketball game. And the showdown at Kfar Maimon appeared more a surrender by an outmaneuvered "army" than a voluntary abandonment of plans to swarm into Gaza.

A second factor was the steady political support Sharon's plan enjoyed throughout the entire period. The Israeli press was overwhelmingly on his side. Nearly all polls showed support for the pullout hovering around 57 percent throughout the entire period.[26] Some on the orange side described a shift during the campaign where more Israeli Arabs came to favor the pullout while

---

25. In Jewish mysticism, a curse upon a sinner.

26. See, for example, Agence France Presse—English, "Most Israelis Support Gaza Withdrawal: Poll," *Agence France Presse*, July 18, 2005; UPI Correspondents, "Israelis' Support for Pullback Increases," *UPI*, July 1, 2005; and UPI Correspondents, "Smaller Majority Still Favors Pullouts," *UPI*, June 10, 2005.

Table 1. List of Israeli Fatalities Attributable to Terrorism

Year	Fatalities
2001	235
2002	451
2003	210
2004	120
2005	60
(through 31 July)	

Source: Interview with Avi Dichter, Tel Aviv, August 1, 2005.

more Israeli Jews opposed it. This mirrored Palestinian sentiment on the West Bank and Gaza where even the initially skeptical came to view the pullout as a net gain, regardless of Sharon's motives.[27] Still, it appears that a majority of Israeli Jews, both on the street and in the Knesset, favored the withdrawal. A few months later, this would be reflected in the early rush of support for Kadima, the party Sharon established after leaving the Likud in November 2005.

The third factor was an improving security situation, particularly on the West Bank. In turn, this fueled a sense of optimism about the wall and the general security regime that would follow the pullout. The critical vote in the Knesset came on June 6, 2004 in the midst of this upswing; such favorable security trends were evident both before that vote and before a later implementation resolution. Table 1 displays the list of Israeli fatalities attributable to terrorism compiled by former Shin Bet director Avi Dichter; the vast majority of Israeli fatalities came from suicide bombers.[28]

Dichter claimed that when Operation Defensive Shield, launched in June 2002, permitted him to set up shop in the West Bank, terrorist leaders were spending 90 percent of their time

27. Data provided by the Palestine Center for Policy and Survey Research at www.pcpsr.org/survey/index.html, accessed January 9, 2006.

28. Interview with Dichter.

planning attacks and 10 percent providing for their own security. Palestinian security forces, established in large measure to combat terrorism, were openly fighting alongside the terrorists. Leaders like Marwan Barghouti organized terrorist forces from the remnants of the quasi-official PA militia, Tanzim.

Per his own estimate, Dichter's efforts—using targeted killings against those known to have been involved in planning or executing deadly attacks, developing a network of reliable informers, vastly improving intelligence, skillfully interrogating arrested terrorism suspects, restricting the ease of Palestinian movements with checkpoints and patrols, dismantling Palestinian militias and security forces, and taking advantage of the security fence to track and prevent violations of the Israeli border—reversed the way terrorist leaders budgeted their time. Personal security now came first, with the planning and execution of attacks relegated to the back burner out of sheer necessity.[29]

One can debate many things about Israeli counterterrorism techniques, but unlike the United States in Iraq, Sri Lanka against the Tamil Tigers, and Colombia against FARC, the Israeli approach worked. Israel "won" by changing the background conditions of the operating environment. Moreover it worked without the murderous excess with which Saddam addressed his Shiites or Asad his Hama foes. And with the decline in terror-related deaths and injuries came renewed confidence in the Sharon approach, confidence that translated seamlessly to support for his unilateral disengagement.

Fourth, the one man who might have mobilized national opposition to the Sharon plan, Finance Minister and former prime minister Binyamin (Bibi) Netanyahu, never really got into the fray until it was too late to be seen as anything other than a political opportunist. Indeed, by the time evacuation day arrived, Netan-

---

29. Ibid.

yahu could well have been mistaken for a well-known Democrat who explained his vote against funding for Iraq with the words, "I voted against it. But before that I voted for it."

In fairness, Netanyahu had been doing important work at the Ministry of Finance and had been doing it well. A self-declared "Reaganite-Thatcherite," he was a champion of privatization, selling off big banks, the telephone company Bezek, and the national airline, El Al. He had also cut the welfare rolls, which, along with defense spending cuts, had trimmed the deficit as a percent of GDP from 6.5 to 4.3 in just two years. Small wonder he had been heralded in *Fortune* magazine as a modern public sector economic manager who had helped his country's economy rebound from the Intifada-induced slump to the sort of high-tech heaven that had put Tel Aviv in the same class as South Beach or Santa Monica. Netanyahu's economic program was important enough to him that on at least one occasion he had traded Sharon's backing for his support for the pullout.[30]

Yet on the very eve of the final cabinet vote authorizing commencement of the evacuation, Netanyahu broke ranks, giving an interview to the *Jerusalem Post* in which he came out totally against the withdrawal while insisting he would remain in the cabinet in order to complete his important work.[31] Netanyahu's grounds were succinct. For one thing, he did not like unilateral concessions in principle, particularly after a long anti-terrorist campaign. "This withdrawal is taking place under terrorist pressure," he complained, from which the leaders of Hamas and Islamic Jihad would conclude that terrorism pays.[32] Already an extra NIS 300 million (4.362 was the NIS/dollar exchange rate on January 15, 2006) had been allocated to shore up defenses in the

30. Nelson D. Schwartz, "Prosperity without Peace," *Fortune*, June 13, 2005.
31. Caroline B. Glick, "Why Is Bibi Still in the Government?" *Jerusalem Post*, August 5, 2005.
32. Ibid.

Negev, due to a "realistic possibility" that the security situation there would soon get worse.

Additionally, Netanyahu said that yielding control of the Philadelphia Corridor running along the border between Gaza and Egypt would open the area to weapons smuggling. This observation notably ignored the fact that Israelis had themselves not found a way to stop smuggling through a series of tunnels going under or around the Rafah checkpoint. If *he* were in charge, apparently this would not be an issue. The Palestinians would also use ports for weapons smuggling, Netanyahu warned. "Now there will be a Karine A, a Karine B, Karine C and Gaza will be transformed into a base for Islamic terrorism adjacent to the coast of the State of Israel," he claimed.[33]

Netanyahu's views on Abu Mazen did not seem to differ materially from those of Sharon. It was good to see the Palestinian leader renounce terrorism, but frustrating to see his squeamishness about tackling Hamas and the other terrorist groups, and frustrating to hear him continue to insist on the right of return. "He isn't as terrible as Arafat because he does not actively support terrorism, but he doesn't fulfill the other criteria," said Netanyahu, words that could just as easily have come from the mouth of Sharon.[34] But where Sharon opted to take unilateral steps, Netanyahu—ever the hard-liner—would have devoted his energies to perpetuating the status quo.

To no one's surprise, Netanyahu was out of the cabinet by the time it next met. He and Sharon had some big matters to settle but the dispute would have to wait until after the withdrawal, when Sharon would leave the Likud and Netanyahu would become its candidate for the March 2006 election. This defining struggle between two political heavyweights ended even before it began with Sharon's stroke of January 4.

33. Ibid.
34. Ibid.

Fifth and finally, Sharon's move earned him exactly the support he sought from the Bush administration, providing him with an opening within the spirit, if not the framework, of the Road Map. The highest immediate priority became making sure the withdrawal went smoothly and with little or no violence from the Palestinian side, including Hamas, Islamic Jihad, and the al-Aqsa Martyr's Brigade. The parties also paid some attention to "day after" issues: disposing of the homes and greenhouses and fixtures to be left behind; determining how the checkpoint regime between Egypt and Gaza would work; providing for access between Gaza and the West Bank; deciding how many Gaza residents would be permitted to work in Israel; settling issues relating to the joint custom regime. Trying to resurrect the actual Road Map could wait, affording Sharon needed political breathing space.

Sharon also sought and received support from President Bush on critical final status issues. In an exchange of letters in April of 2004, Mr. Bush offered some long-desired statements on how the United States would interpret UN Security Council Resolutions 242 and 338 as regards Israeli settlement blocs outside the Green Line:

> In light of new realities on the ground, including already existing major Israeli population centers, it is unrealistic to expect that the outcome of final status negotiations will be a full and complete return to the armistice lines of 1949, and all previous efforts to negotiate a two-state solution have reached the same conclusion. It is realistic to expect that any final status agreement will only be achieved on the basis of mutually agreed changes that reflect these realities.[35]

Sharon would soon embarrass his benefactor by claiming that

35. David Makovsky, *Engagement through Disengagement* (Washington: Washington Institute for Near East Policy, 2005), Appendix 8, "Exchange of Letters between Prime Minister Sharon and President Bush, April 2004," 116–120.

the president's words meant that the United States accepted the three large settlement blocs—Ariel, Gush Etzion, and Ma'aleh Adumim—as part of Israel. Red-faced U.S. diplomats tried to explain that the letter carried no weight as a formal statement of U.S. policy and that the president was not seeking to resolve specific issues.

At a joint White House press conference on April 14, 2004, the president interpreted the security wall in a way that made it acceptable within the framework of the Road Map: "The barrier being erected by Israel as part of that security effort should, as your government has stated, be a security rather than a political barrier. It should be temporary rather than permanent, and therefore not prejudice any final status issues, including final borders."[36]

Sharon could not have asked for more supportive words as they put the United States squarely on Israel's side of an advisory case on the security barrier being heard at the Hague's International Court of Justice. In that most unfriendly venue, Israel would later be found to have erected the wall as a political rather than a national security barrier since there was no Palestinian state and thus no need for a national security measure to protect against its incursions. This was, of course, the essence of judicial cynicism. If there was no threat from the Palestinians, where were all those Qassam rockets and plastic suicide bombs coming from? And who was killing all those civilians? Had the court's reasoning been applied to the September 11 attacks, no retaliatory action by the United States would have been justified because the nineteen terrorists represented no particular nation.

Finally, at that April press conference, Sharon obtained from Mr. Bush the most direct presidential statement ever dealing with the issue of the Palestinian right of return:

36. David Makovsky, supra, Appendix 9, "Excerpts from Joint Bush-Sharon Press Conference, White House, April 14, 2004," pp. 123–125.

It seems clear that an agreed, just, fair and realistic framework
for a solution to the Palestinian refugee issue as part of any
final status agreement will need to be found through the establishment of a Palestinian state and the settling of Palestinian
refugees there rather than Israel.

No Israeli leader ever enjoyed such a level of support from
an American president. In a dazzling display of friendship, the
president had accepted the wall and put a favorable spin on its
purpose, read Yasser Arafat out of the negotiation game, embraced the idea of settlements outside the Green Line remaining
in Israeli hands, and took a stand on the right of return that could
have been (and may have been) drafted by the prime minister's
office. Sharon would soon win three critical votes in the disengagement process, the first approving the unilateral disengagement plan; the second, authorization by his Likud Party for a
coalition agreement with Labor; and the third, permitting the
withdrawal to begin. He was riding high.

4. The Palestinian Moderates

DR. EYAD SARAJ gets more attention from the western press than his political influence would warrant. A chain-smoking Gaza psychiatrist with a humanist outlook on domestic and international matters, he talks of entering the political arena as a "third force" between the corruption of Fatah and the Islamic extremism of Hamas. He offers little, however, to inspire any confidence that he has found many potential constituents in this deeply bifurcated society, let alone developed an organization capable of getting them to the polls. His powerlessness is underlined by reports that he has been arrested and tortured on three occasions. Yet his mind is so sharp, his eye so keen, his moral courage so daunting, and his voice so clear that reporters find him too attractive to ignore.

On a Saturday morning in late July, he held forth on a dock beside the Mediterranean as he prepared to launch his twenty-nine-foot inboard. "So this was a very good opportunity for us and unfortunately it was completely destroyed," he said, referring to the decade of rule by the Fatah-dominated PA beginning with Arafat's 1994 return. "Because suddenly the elite of the PLO and Fatah took over, which proved over the years to be absolutely distant from the rule of law, from democracy, and they proved also to be not very good managers, even at the low level."[1]

The imminent Israeli pullout from Gaza had given rise to

1. Eyad Saraj, transcript of interview with author, Gaza, July 30, 2005.

some public talk of a victory vindicating all the bloodshed. Saraj
would have none of it. As he emphasized:

> No, I think they lost miserably. I think Palestinians proved to
> be the worst of their enemies. Who gained is Hamas. Hamas
> gained. But the rest of the society, the Palestinians in general,
> the Palestinian cause, the just cause was damaged. The peace
> process was damaged, the peace camp in Israel was destroyed,
> the Palestinian Authority was weakened, the whole focus in the
> world became fighting terror and we Palestinians became some-
> how part of this terrorist structure so that just cause, which
> should have been the higher moral cause was dimmed to a ques-
> tion between security and terror.[2]

Saraj was substantially right on both counts. A senior western
diplomat estimated that had the Second Intifada been scored like
a sporting match on a ten-point system, the Israelis might have
gotten an eight on the military side and a five on the politics,
with the Palestinians scoring four on the military side and zero
on politics.[3] "Sharon had the advantage as long as this was a fight
in the alley," the diplomat said. "At the negotiating table, with
international support, the PA had the advantage. Arafat either
didn't know this, or didn't care. He was the road block."[4]

On the day the Second Intifada erupted and continuing for
several months thereafter, the Palestinians had within their grasp
a state with a capital in East Jerusalem together with 97 percent
of the West Bank and all of the Gaza Strip. Already they presided
over areas in which more than 90 percent of the Palestinian population resided. Every day tens of thousands crossed the borders
for work in Israel. Travel between Gaza and the West Bank was
possible, as was overseas travel. With the establishment of dip-

---

2. Ibid.
3. Interview with senior western diplomat, July 22, 2005.
4. Ibid.

lomatic relations, Jordan too had become readily accessible and a purchaser of Palestinian goods.

Now the Palestinians were paying a surtax for their terrorism in the form of a pervasive military presence, checkpoints, curfews, severe travel restrictions, and the construction of a "security fence" that was swallowing up 8.6 percent of the West Bank with thousands of West Bank residents caught in the "seam" or "security zone" between the 1967 borders and the fence. Thousands of others were blocked from previously accessible land.

A good way to tell which side prevailed in the military contest is to note which side occupies whose territory and which is issuing the orders that must be obeyed. In their essay in the French paper *Le Monde*, Robert Malley, a former Middle East specialist on Bill Clinton's NSC, and Hussein Agha of Saint Anthony's College, Oxford—neither of them sympathetic to Israel—make the telling point that Sharon won the current round of the Israeli-Palestinian conflict by imposing such difficult conditions that he succeeded in "diverting the Palestinian's concentration from political issues to mundane matters of more immediate, quotidian concern. He appears to have achieved this ambition, an outcome Abu Mazen long predicted, which is why at the very outset of the armed Intifada in 2000 he called for it to end."[5] In this new situation, Israel holds all of the cards.

Saraj was also right with respect to the Palestinian domestic circumstances. Arafat returned from his lengthy exile bringing the authoritarian habits that had served him well running his organization from foreign bases first located in Jordan, then Lebanon, and, finally, Tunisia. He controlled the purse strings of the movement, divided responsibility for security among at least thirteen

5. Hussein Agha and Robert Malley, "Abu Mazen: Palestine's Last Best Hope," *Le Monde Diplomatique*, February 2005. Agha and Malley make a similar argument in the *New York Review of Books*: see Agha and Malley, "The Lost Palestinians," *New York Review of Books* 52, no. 10 (June 2005).

factions, permitted no legislative oversight, established no independent judiciary, and permitted even so able a top lieutenant as Muhammad Dahlan to funnel millions from his control over concrete and oil monopolies into his own pockets. He eliminated anything resembling academic freedom at such proud universities as Birzeit and an-Najah and provided health, welfare, and municipal services at levels so lacking as to invite Hamas and other nonstate organizations with political agendas of their own to gain a foothold.

Yet Arafat the "Old Man" personified the Palestinian cause to the extent that so long as he lived he was impervious to challenge. When he died, the sins of the father were visited upon his political progeny. Qais Abdul-Karim, the head of the Democratic Front for the Liberation of Palestine and member of the PLO Central Council explained:

> People have had enough of a Palestinian Authority that is monopolized by Fatah. People have had enough of corruption in the Palestinian authority, which devours a major portion of the resources that this PNA could master [. . .] Instead of going in the direction of alleviating the hardships and the suffering of the people, they go to the elite and all their privileges and corruption.[6]

Arafat's death in November 2004 provided a window for reform, thereby leading to Abu Mazen's election. His goal was to restore the credibility of the Palestinian march toward nationhood, making the world and particularly the United States view the Palestinian cause with renewed sympathy. To achieve this outcome, as Malley and Agha offer, "Palestinians must stabilize the situation, restore law and order, rein in all armed militias, build transpar-

---

6. Qais Abdul-Karim, transcript of interview with author, Ramallah, July 29 2005.

ent, legitimate centralized institutions, and above all, cease armed attacks against Israel."[7]

Palestinian elites viewed Israel's decision to withdraw from Gaza with mixed emotions. Revealed in stages throughout 2003 and 2004, the withdrawal could be viewed as a product of the Intifada, perhaps its most visible achievement. On the other hand, the elites appreciated that many other factors contributed to the decision, including Sharon's desire to stifle pressure from the United States and Europe to return to the negotiating table and the possibility that he would use the period of grace following the pullout to literally cement Israel's hold on the West Bank and East Jerusalem. In terms of their own interests, Palestinian leaders needed cooperation from the Israelis vis-à-vis facilitating both human and commercial traffic from the territory, supervision of the Philadelphia corridor running along Gaza's border with Egypt, resuming flights from Gaza's airport, lifting a six-mile Israeli-imposed restriction on sea traffic from Gaza, commencing work on a commercial port, and myriad other practical issues. Regarding the oft-remarked "day after" the Israeli pullout, mainstream Palestinian leaders hoped Gaza's residents would find themselves in something other than a "prison" holding 1.3 million inmates.

Yet another consideration was the Palestinian hope that Israel would see assistance to Abu Mazen and other moderates as in its own enlightened self-interest. Lacking any core constituency of his own, Abu Mazen's one hope of retaining influence while subduing Hamas and other radical factions was to cultivate an impression among Palestinians that he could deliver a bilateral relationship with Israel making their lives more bearable—economically and otherwise. This meant not only cooperation on the above list of Gaza-related issues, but such others as prisoner release, eased travel and related restrictions on the West Bank,

7. See Agha and Malley, "Last Best Hope."

construction of the wall in ways that minimized its impact on daily Palestinian life, and the demonstration of some inclination toward participating in an accelerated peace process. Abu Mazen had already secured a *tahdiya*, a period of calm or cease-fire, from Hamas, but lacked the muscle—or thought he did—to either disarm Hamas and other radical organizations or compel them to integrate their own militias into a single security force controlled by the Palestinian Authority. Instead, his instincts were to keep Hamas quiet through negotiation and wait until the legislative council elections of January 25, 2006, when the political strength of the various factions would be sorted out. Then, perhaps, the ideal of "one authority, one gun, one law" might be achievable. Like most observers of the unfolding political story, Abu Mazen assumed Hamas would win enough seats to have its maturity tested but not enough to wield real political power. That proved to be a misjudgment of cosmic proportions. Had Abu Mazen fully appreciated the extent of the Hamas political threat, he could have insisted that as the price for full participation in the political process Hamas renounce terrorism, disband its militia and agree to abide by such past government-to-government agreements as Oslo. There would have been broad international support for such a requirement, but Abu Mazen in effect placed consensus ahead of order and wound up with neither.

All things considered, the Palestinian leadership resolved to treat the Israeli withdrawal to the 1967 borders as a positive thing, to commit itself—a commitment shared by Hamas—to avoid taking any action, such as violence against departing settlers or evacuating troops, that would embarrass the Israelis or invite reprisal, and to convey a sense of moderation in commenting on Sharon and his motives. Most of all, Abu Mazen treated the event as a test of his ability to bring the Palestinians back to the point where they proved themselves worthy of statehood and a negotiated peace process. Ahmad Abd Alrahman, a close friend of Arafat and senior Fatah figure, described Abu Mazen's plans weeks before the pullout:

> Our President Abbas will stay all the time in Gaza until the withdrawal. It means we are serious to do our assignment in Gaza Strip. The assignment is law and order and security, and no violation of the agreement. I mean, no rockets, no any kind of violence against the Israelis in the Green Line. It is part of Israel, it is part of the state of Israel, we recognize Israel as a state.[8]

Yet as it became clear that Sharon had no intention of extending political help to the PA leadership, Palestinian sentiments turned bitter. For example, Mohammed Dahlan, the young Fatah power in Gaza who may one day inherit Arafat's khafia, said in an interview with *Haaretz Magazine*:

> The only thing he can do is to give the Palestinians hope. Sharon is not giving any hope, he is continuing to build the fence, he is expanding the settlements and telling the Palestinians that they have two options: either to die from this life, or to die from the tanks. There is no hope for the students, there is no hope for the future generation.[9]

On the topic of whether Sharon deserves any credit for the pullback, Dahlan was clear:

> Of course not. That's Sharon's strategy. He declared that he wants to leave Gaza in order to continue the occupation in the West Bank and to strengthen the settlements, he promised the settlers in the West Bank that they have nothing to worry about. That's no secret. We believe every word Sharon says. Every word of his is the truth; there is no Palestinian state, there is no peace process, there are no negotiations.[10]

---

8. Ahmad Abd Alrahman, transcript of interview with author, Ramallah, July 29, 2005.

9. Gideon Levy, "Get Out of Our Lives," *Haaretz Magazine*, July 22, 2005.

10. Ibid.

Some Palestinian voices were less resentful, more pleading in tone. Smoking heavy-smelling cigarettes and sipping Arab coffee in his Ramallah office, his hair dyed jet-black, Ahmad Abd Alrahman lamented Sharon's tendency to build roadblocks rather than bridges to Abu Mazen: "Sharon said over time while Arafat was alive that we do not have a partner. Now I am saying that we have no partner from the Israeli side. The Palestinian side is ready—I mean Abu Mazen, who has the decision in his hand. He is ready, and he is not playing games, but where are the Israelis?"[11]

The ride from Jerusalem to Jericho is perilous. Steep sandy mountains give way to deep wadis and valleys hundreds of feet below. The paved roads are barely wide enough for two vehicles. The hairpin turns provide an instant cure for heat-induced ennui. There is no guardrail. Here and there the Israeli traffic administrators have deployed warning signs consisting of a black exclamation point on an orange background. The city is the lowest on earth and, with a history exceeding six thousand years, the longest continuously habited. On the town's main street, in a pleasant villa that serves as both office and home, lives Saeb Erakat. Dapper, very smart, well practiced in the science of diplomacy, Erakat can often be found fine-tuning Palestinian negotiating positions while issuing directions to subordinates. They, in turn, are busy refining arguments supporting the position taken, marshalling information about the latest confrontation or dispute with the Israelis, keeping tabs on anything that might make the Palestinians look reasonable and the Israelis, hard-line and close-minded.

Palestinian public relations have become infinitely more professional since Camp David where Barak and his colleagues—aided by President Clinton and his devoted Middle East aide Dennis Ross—successfully portrayed themselves as daring adven-

---

11. Interview with Alrahman.

turers for peace and Arafat as negative, unprepared, and uncompromising. Now the Palestinians translate their ideas into formal positions described in literature designed to catch the western eye. Backing them is a Negotiation Support Unit comprised largely of young American lawyers, economists, and public relations specialists who are the sons and daughters of Palestinian émigrés.

Their work product is not perfect, as one handout entitled "The Sex Month Report of Israeli Violations" clearly demonstrates. Yet for an understanding of where the Palestinians currently stand on the right of return, Jerusalem, or border issues, for an accounting of their difficulties with the wall, or their complaints regarding checkpoints, the de facto grabbing of West Bank property, Israel's failure to deal promptly with illegal outposts, or an inadequate loosening of the grip on Gaza, the Negotiation Support Unit makes an enormous contribution.

Like most of the Palestinian elite, Erakat had little good to say about Israeli unilateralism. "The question is one of demography for them, not geography," he claimed. "They want to solve their problems—get rid of 1.3 million Palestinians so that you can maintain whatever you want in the settlements in the West Bank."[12] Erakat dismissed the claims of unilateral disengagement supporters who say the country was forced into the approach by the absence of a Palestinian partner. Rather, he argued, the purpose is to move in a way that lowers Palestinian expectations. "They can snatch a piece of land in the north of the West Bank, Jerusalem, Ma'aleh Adumim, Gush Etzion, and then the Palestinians just have to accept. What this will do is kill Abu Mazen, kill Saeb Erakat, kill the Palestinian moderate camp, and end up supporting the extremists, which will translate to victories for other extremists in this region."[13]

12. Saeb Erakat, transcript of interview with author, Jericho, August 6, 2005.
13. Ibid.

Erakat was twenty-three years old in 1967 when Israel first occupied Jericho. Now he has four children, including twenty-three-year-old twin girls, and spoke darkly of having grandchildren also born under occupation, blocked by a wall from traveling their land freely. He claimed Israel is empowered by U.S. backing while Americans look at this part of the world and wonder why they are hated. "We don't hate you," he said. "We come to you for help. We want democracy, we want freedom, we want liberty, we want the rule of law, we want transparency. That's what Palestinians are all about."[14]

Erakat's assistants assembled a collection of Palestinian positions on final status issues and a separate illustrated soft-covered booklet on the wall. The handout on refugees consists of six single-spaced pages, including one directing readers to other resources on the issue.[15] The first five pages follow a question-and-answer format, detailing fifteen questions addressing such matters as the origin of the problem, the current number (6.5 million) and distribution of refugees, their legal status, and the partial text of UN Resolution 194, passed in December 1948 and calling for the right of return home for those "refugees wishing to return to their homes and live at peace with their neighbors."[16]

It is the Palestinian position, consistently advanced at Camp David, Taba, and even today, that Resolution 194 has lost none of its bite and that, with some allowance for human logistics, all those refugees wishing to return to Israel have the right to do so, although the handout seeks to finesse through evasion and dis-

14. Ibid.

15. PLO Negotiations Support Unit, "Palestinian Refugees," PLO Negotiations Affairs Department. Available online at www.nad-plo.org.

16. United Nations General Assembly Resolution 194, A/RES/194, December 11 1948. Available online at http://domino.un.org/unispal.nsf/0/c758572 b78d1cd0085256bcf0077e51a?OpenDocument.

traction the problem of two Arab majorities in two states folding in an historical instant into one.[17]

Furthermore, the Palestinian position runs roughshod over the Israeli concern that acknowledging a right of return threatens the Jewish nature of Israel. Significantly, the Negotiating Unit contends that the "end of religious/ethnic discrimination with respect to the right of return threatens nothing other than discrimination itself." Preserved would be "the Jewish historical attachment to Israel," and "the rights of Jews to immigrate to Israel." The right of return "seeks only to address historic injustices." Of course, the Israel that defines this "attachment" and that has attracted these immigrants is a Jewish Israel. The Palestinian formula is thus the complete negation of the two-state solution. It is a formula for the extinction of Israel as a Jewish state, as perfect in its extremism as is the advocacy of Greater Israel enthusiasts for the creation of a Jewish state from the Mediterranean to the Jordan with the presence of four to five million Palestinians as little more than a logistical inconvenience. In both cases, the existing populations—with roots, economic livelihoods, and political structures—are treated as so much old furniture in a "makeover" room.[18]

WHEN I SAT DOWN WITH HER, Hanan Ashwari's first question had to do with the failing health of ABC News anchor Peter Jennings. They had been friends since the 1970s, Peter one of many western journalists who developed early respect and affection for the brilliant and talented lady from Ramallah who could write a novel or deliver a raging polemic with equal facility and conviction. Ashwari hated the Israeli occupation but endorsed a two-state solution at a time when doing so took some courage. She was

17. PLO Negotiations Support Unit, "Palestinian Refugees."
18. Ibid.

close friends with Arafat and yet resented his authoritarian ways. She was an integral part of the First Intifada, often giving voice to her people's discontents from her roving pulpit of network television cameras, but opposed its violent successor "because I believe that things went drastically wrong and I believe that extremists on both sides took over and the people paid the price." As with other Palestinian moderates, she expressed bitterness over the reluctance of the Sharon government to do more for Abu Mazen. "I mean, okay, Abu Mazen has an agenda for peace, of nonviolence, of reform, of moderation. How did they respond to this in Israel? Did they stop their policies? Did they stop their settlement activities? Did they stop the wall? Did they stop assassinations? No, they didn't."[19]

The wall seems to have struck a deeper note of resentment in Ms. Ashwari than in others. Perhaps it offends her poetic soul. Or maybe as a woman—albeit a Christian—in a culture jealous of male prerogatives she has faced walls all her life, climbing one only to confront a new, more foreboding structure. The symbolism was strong. As she eloquently put it:

> To me this is the most viable expression of oppression and of provocation. You are stealing people's land. You are building a wall between their homes and their land. You are building a wall to take away their water. You are building walls surrounding whole communities and villages. You're imprisoning people. You're stealing their horizon. You're turning the West Bank into a prison. It's horrible. It's ugly. I mean to me it is the ultimate expression of not just ugliness, but viciousness. I can't stand this.[20]

Israelis see it differently. When they speak of the wall, they think of it as a system of sensors, a "smart fence"—95 percent of it is fence—packed with the most sophisticated electronic equip-

19. Hanan Ashwari, transcript of interview with author, Jerusalem, July 29, 2005.
20. Ibid.

ment to detect trespassers. A cleared, flat area on the Palestinian side permits Israeli monitors to identify and stop most would-be infiltrators. A similar piece of flattened terrain on the Israeli side is designed to facilitate hot pursuit. Statistics regarding the reduced number of successful infiltrators plus accounts from captured terrorists regarding the wall's influence on their planning combine—even before completion of construction—to persuade even many early skeptics that the wall works.

Palestinian complaints with the wall, expressed in both public relations literature and court arguments, are less emotional than Ms. Ashwari's. Their concerns focus, in the short run, on the great harm inflicted on Palestinian communities and, in the long run, on the wall's effects upon borders and demography. Israeli security could have been achieved, they argue, by dismantling settlements and building the wall inside Israel's 1967 border. Instead, Mr. Sharon cleverly distracted the world's attention by unilaterally taking eight thousand settlers out of Gaza while moving to functionally annex important parts of the West Bank and East Jerusalem, carving up Palestinian areas into dysfunctional cantons in the process. Extending some 763 kilometers—over twice the length of the 1967 border—it will embrace more than 9 percent of the West Bank, an area where, according to Palestinian estimates, two hundred and forty-nine thousand Palestinians—including residents of East Jerusalem—now live.[21] Israelis involved in planning the fence claim the Palestinian figures are wild exaggerations and depend on the creative use of Arab residents of Jerusalem who should not be counted for this purpose. The wall will embrace only 8.6 percent of the West Bank, while the real number of Palestinians caught in its seam—thereby inside the area Israel would now claim—is only about thirty thousand. Still, Palestinians fear that what will be cut off are not Pal-

21. Israel High Court Ruling, Docket H.C.J. 7957/04, International Legality of the Security Fence and Sections near Alfei Menashe, September 15, 2005, p. 6.

estinians from Israel, but Palestinians from their agricultural lands, their hospitals, their children's schools, their places of business, other Palestinians, and ultimately from their putative capital and economic heart, East Jerusalem.[22] They will be cut off from a viable state.

THE ISRAELI THREAT to Jerusalem derives from the wall itself combined with the construction of homes for Jews in East Jerusalem and the on-again, off-again Israeli plans for destruction of what Palestinians fear will be hundreds of their homes. No less ominous is the so-called E-1 (East-1) project, designed to link the Ma'aleh Adumim settlement to Jerusalem "through the construction of three-and-a-half thousand housing units, an industrial park, offices, entertainment and sports centers, ten hotels and a cemetery."[23] Palestinians claim the project will effectively sever East Jerusalem's north-south link to the remainder of the West Bank and increase the population of the already illegal settlement from thirty thousand four hundred Israelis to seventy thousand.[24] The project's planning was begun under Yitzhak Rabin. The Israeli's say yielding the area of planned construction to the Palestinians would block Israel's east-west contiguity from Jerusalem. Even before the Palestinians elected to be run by a Hamas government an Israeli cave-in on E-1 was unlikely. Now funds needed to get the project going will probably be allocated.

In a July 2004 advisory opinion, the International Court of Justice (ICJ) branded the wall contrary to international law and a violation of the human rights of Palestinians. Despite Israel's

22. Palestine Liberation Organization, "Israel's Wall," Negotiations Affairs Department, October 2004.

23. Palestine Liberation Organization, "Israel's Wall (Special Edition: First Anniversary of the International Court of Justice's Ruling on Israel's Wall)," Negotiations Affairs Department, July 9, 2005.

24. Ibid.

claim that the wall is temporary, the ICJ found "that the construction of the wall and its associated regime create a 'fait accompli' on the ground that could well become permanent in which case, and notwithstanding the formal characterization of the wall by Israel, it would be tantamount to de facto annexation."[25]

Yet what of Israel's claim that the wall was necessary for self-defense? In an astonishing bit of reasoning that perhaps reflected more on themselves than the Israelis, the ICJ judges held that as there was no "State of Palestine" occupied by the Palestinians, Israel lacked a legitimate self-defense motive in the wall's construction. This is something of an oxymoron considering that under Article 2 of the Fourth Geneva Convention—the governing document in the case—ICJ jurisdiction would not attach unless an armed conflict existed between two contracting parties. Only once such a condition is met does the Convention apply in territory occupied by one of the parties. As the Israeli Supreme Court would later note wryly of the ICJ, "[t]o achieve its finding, the court held at the same time that there exists an armed conflict, and that territories are occupied territories of another state, but also and at the same time asserted that Israel has no right to defend itself in that conflict, because there is no other state involved."[26] Israel had not participated directly in the case, challenging the court's jurisdiction, and clearly did not consider itself bound by the result.

Palestinian litigants were active in the Israeli courts as well, producing two major Supreme Court decisions that clarified and delineated the strict defensive use of the wall in terms of both practice and legality. The first one was the *Beit Sourik* case, involving clusters of villages running from the Bethlehem area to

25. Advisory Opinion, "Legal Consequences of the Construction of a Wall in the Occupied Palestinian Territory," International Court of Justice, Press Release 2004/28, 9 July 2004.

26. Israel High Court Ruling Docket H.C.J. 7959/04, p. 1, supra.

Samaria; the second involved Palestinian residents of several villages in the vicinity of Alfei Menashe, an Israeli settlement of just
over five thousand in the northern West Bank.[27]

In *Alfei Menashe*, the court first noted that the project was
initially undertaken to defend Israel from the "strategic threat" of
suicide bombings. Its purpose was security. But security does not
stop at the 1967 Green Line. Rather, it extends to areas under
Israel's "belligerent occupation," territories where the military
commander is "the long arm of the state." It is both the right and
the duty of that commander to offer protection to residents of
and visitors to that territory, even those who are there illegally.
Can the military commander order that the fence follow a particular route? "In the *Beit Sourik Case* our answer was that the military commander is not authorized to order the construction of a
separation fence, if the reason behind the fence is a political goal
of 'annexing' territories of the area to the State of Israel." Moreover, "construction of the fence does not involve transfer of the
ownership on which it is built," implying that if and when the
fence is removed all rights to the land revert to its owner.[28] This
interpretation of the law was entirely consistent with earlier holdings of the court denying the right of military commanders to
construct roads for the purpose of serving the convenience of Israeli commuters or reflecting a political desire for Israelis to occupy all of the area of biblical Israel.

The inquiry did not end with a finding by the court that the
military commander was motivated by appropriate security concerns in selecting the route of the fence and thus demarking the
security zone or "seam" behind it. As the court stated in *Beit Sourik*:

27. Israeli Supreme Court Judgment Regarding the Security Fence, June 24,
2004, *Beit Sourik*. Available online via the Jewish Virtual Library at: www
.jewishvirtuallibrary.org/jsource/peace/fencect.html.
    28. Israel High Court Ruling Docket H.C.J. 7957/04, supra., p. 10.

The law of war usually creates a delicate balance between two poles: military necessity on one hand and humanitarian considerations on the other [. . .] The obligations and rights of a military administration are defined, on the one hand, by its own military needs and, on the other, by the need to ensure, to the extent possible, the normal daily life of the population.[29]

In *Beit Sourik*, the court moved to establish a test of what it termed "proportionality," required of the military in each act affecting local populations. And this in turn requires the military commander to satisfy three subtests. First, "the objective must be related to the means." If you are situating a fence in such a way that access to agricultural land, schools, medical facilities, or roads is impeded, there must be a rational connection between that action and the desired enhancement in security. Second, in "the spectrum of means that can be used to achieve the objective, the least injurious means must be used."[30] Finally, the third test represents a narrow application of proportionality in that it requires that the specific damage caused to the resident population "must be of proper proportion to the gain brought about by that means."[31] Great inconvenience cannot be justified if the security enhancement is modest, even if the nexus between the inconvenience and security improvement is real and the steps taken to further security are the least injurious available.

Cumulatively, the court invoked the third test (local proportionality) and struck down the military commander's action with respect to every village, ordering revisions to the wall's planned route. It calculated that doing nothing would cut off more than thirteen thousand farmers from their lands and from tens of thousands of their trees. Gates leading to the agricultural lands would be open only at designated times, permitting entrance only

29. *Beit Sourik,* supra. p. 29.
30. *Beit Sourik,* supra. p. 20.
31. Ibid.

to those with special licenses. The result would be long lines and a substantial economic inconvenience, far out of proportion to any enhancement in security. The court ruled that the action violated both the Hague regulations and the Fourth Geneva Convention. It ordered substantial changes in the route of the security fence. By the Palestinians' own calculations, Beit Sourik went from 76 percent of its land designated for the security area inside the fence to 15 percent, Biddu from 45 percent to 27 percent, Beit Liqya from 27 percent to 5 percent, and so on.[32] Particularly noteworthy was the intervention of groups representing Israeli peace activists, including residents of Mevasseret Tzion—one of those the original plan was designed to protect—who said the military order would detract from their security by enraging Palestinians with whom they now got along well but who would be severely hurt by the fence.

One year later, on September 15, 2005, the court granted similar relief to Palestinians affected by the proposed security fence route in the area of Alfei Menashe. Once again the decision was based on proportionality as the degree of injury to Palestinian residents was far greater than the marginal improvement in security for the resident population.

To the reporter traveling the West Bank, the perceptions of Hanan Ashwari seem more grounded in daily human experience than are the Israeli Supreme Court's notions of proportionality, though it is certainly the case that the checkpoints, rather than the security barrier, are the major impediments to mobility. The ten-minute drive from Ramallah to Jerusalem can take two hours or more when things get clogged at the Qalandiya checkpoint. The landscape is dotted by Palestinians traveling on foot over rural hills from village to town and back again. A separate "temporary" fence snakes out from Ariel like fingers trying to catch

32. PLO, "Israel's Wall," July 9, 2005, supra., p. 24.

one Jewish settlement or another, making it tough if not impossible for neighboring Palestinian villagers to use the land efficiently. Decorating the wall with graffiti comparing the Israelis to Hitler, listing grievances on it, or painting escapist landscapes or billowy clouds has become the fashion. All the while, complain the Palestinians, Israelis say they need a wall to provide security, simultaneously closing their eyes to provocative settlements and outposts dotting every hilltop, way beyond the reach of any security rationale, providing the potential for a dramatic change in the delicate situation

Israel does plan to ease congestion at Qalandiya and other jammed gateways by converting the facilities into civilian-manned checkpoints accessible through computerized identity cards.[33] At the end of the day, however, their collective motto seems to be, "Life over the quality of life."

In a larger sense, one retains hope for a society that observes a rule of law, where a few men and women in robes can change the configuration of a wall because it was insufficiently respectful of the rights of people who just months ago were cheering and supporting the "martyrs" trying to bring Israel to its knees with waves of terrorist attacks. Now the moderate Palestinians say they want peace. They accept two states. Some want material support in the security area so they can fight some tough opponents of peace. Others argue political support is even more important. Lift the restrictions on mobility, they were pleading only a few months ago. Let our people out of jail. Let us talk about the ultimate issues. We can deliver the settlement we both must seek only if we are credible in our own community. And for that, you hold the key.

Then the Palestinian masses elected a Hamas government and

---

33. Steven Erlanger, "Israel Is Easing Barrier Burden, but Palestinians Still See a Border," *New York Times*, December 22, 2005.

the finger-pointing started all over again. One first wonders about the veracity of the claims made by the Palestinian moderates regarding the desire for peace among the Palestinians. A still bigger question is what is to be the fate of the Palestinian moderates now that they have been voted out of office. That is, if Hamas—a radical organization—has been voted into power and the moderates voted out, will the moderates change their political views in order to retain influence? Or will the "moderates" take up arms, this time against a Hamas-led government.

Many Israelis would like to have helped Abu Mazen and his "moderate Palestinians" if and when either he or they could have identified them. But they say they learned some things from the Second Intifada that they will not soon forget. First, do not strengthen your foe until you are sure he is your foe no longer. As a corollary, actions still speak louder than words. Stating you are a partner does not make you one; specific actions are called for, not declarations alone. Finally, where the trade-off is between security and benevolence, err on the side of security.

Now with a Hamas government, the issue of bilateral talks is moot and the question of unilateral disengagement is more central than ever before. Those continuing to embrace the doctrine have the opportunity to do so in its purest form—when there truly is no negotiating partner. No longer does the elected Palestinian majority offer peace at the end of a negotiating process. The Hamas charter calls only for war.

5. Hamas and Kin: The Terrorists

ON APRIL 12, 2002, Sheikh Ibrihim Madhi of the Palestinian Authority delivered a widely broadcast sermon at the Sheikh Ijlin Mosque in Gaza City in which he embraced the call for genocide against the Jewish people. Citing a *hadith* (narration of religious teachings) familiar to many Moslems he recited: "The Day of Judgment will not come about until Moslems fight Jews (killing the Jews), when the Jew will hide behind stones and trees. The stones and trees will say, O Moslems, O Abdullah, there is a Jew behind me, come and kill him."[1] The same hadith appears in Article Seven of the 1988 covenant through which a radical Islamic group calling itself the Islamic Resistance Movement—also known as Hamas—declared its existence. It was the unwillingness or inability of Fatah and the PA to move boldly against Hamas during the Second Intifada, instead, then and later, pursuing a policy of appeasement that gave Hamas the chance to seize political power through the ballot box, delaying indefinitely the commencement of serious negotiations aimed at resolving the Israeli-Palestinian dispute.

Two years before Sheikh Madhi's sermon, the PA—for purposes of conducting Intifada 2—made a de facto alliance with Hamas, widely viewed even in the Palestinian community as a terrorist organization. Its covenant oozes hatred for the Jews and reeks with the stench of blood libel. It claims, for example, that

1. USC-MSA Compendium of Muslim Texts, "Sunnah and Hadith." Available online at www.usc.edu/dept/MSA/fundamentals/hadithsunnah/.

Jews were behind the French and Communist revolutions, mas-
terminded the First World War, and orchestrated the destruction
of the Islamic Caliphate. "Additionally, Jews were behind World
War II, through which they made huge financial gains by trading
in armaments, and paved the way for the establishment of their
state."[2] In Hamas' eyes, the danger is of paramount importance
simply because Jews aspire first to control all the land from the
Nile to the Euphrates rivers and then expand even further, a plan
embodied in the "Protocols of the Elders of Zion" and of which
"their present conduct is the best proof of what we are saying."[3]

The remedy is, accordingly, war, one in which "Israel will
exist and will continue to exist until Islam will obliterate it, just
as it obliterated others before it." By proxy, "there is no solution
for the Palestinian question except through Jihad; diplomacy and
peace treaties are all a waste of time and vain endeavors."

In addition to the extinction of Israel, Hamas has a second
strategic objective directly related to the first: the development
of Palestine as an Islamic state. Its covenant, rooted in Islamic
law and tradition, stands in direct contrast to the secular PLO
"National Covenant." Based upon its past record and role in the
Palestinian community, it is today by far the largest, best fi-
nanced, and most politically active of the Palestinian terrorist organizations. And as corruption, cronyism, and the inability to provide law and order or to win compassionate treatment from Israel
have brought the Fatah-dominated PA to its knees, Hamas demonstrated its strength by successsfully contesting local elections
before winning an outright majority in the Palestine Legislative
Council.

Hamas is an offshoot of the Palestinian Muslim Brotherhood,

2. "The Covenant of the Islamic Resistance Movement," 18 August 1988.
Available online via the Avalon Project at Yale Law School at www.yale.edu/
lawweb/avalon/mideast/hamas.htm.
    3. Ibid.

itself a spin-off from the parent Egyptian movement. The original Muslim Brotherhood was a leading advocate of fundamentalist Islam and purveyor of the need for jihad throughout the Muslim world. Its Palestinian branch was formed in 1946 and evolved into a virulently anti-Israel force. Predicated upon this dual tradition of anti-Israeli and Islamic fervor, Hamas' immediate predecessor was a group known as Al-Mujamma Al-Islami (Islamic Association), formed in 1973 by the wheelchair-bound Shiekh Ahmed Yassin.

Regarded by his followers as both a spiritual and political leader, it was under Yassin's guidance that Al-Mujamma Al-Islami developed a system known as Da'wah, a massive social, religious, educational, cultural, and medical infrastructure throughout the territories. It registered as a charity in Israel in 1978 and received covert assistance from the Israelis, who were anxious to see groups develop that would drain support from the PLO. With hindsight, this would prove too easy for Israel's own good as Yasser Arafat and his longtime associates became increasingly isolated from the PLO's West Bank and Gaza constituents during their twelve-year sojourn in Tunisia.

Operating mainly from their base at the Islamic University of Gaza, Al-Mujamma began testing its muscle and developing a following. At the time its principal targets were those it felt were disseminating values antithetical to Islam in the Occupied Territories, a group including proprietors of cinemas, casinos, and liquor stores. When, during the First Intifada, the newly named Hamas began killing Israeli soldiers, Israel responded by arresting Yassin. He was released in 1997 by Prime Minister Netanyahu at the insistence of Jordan's king Hussein after the Mosad embarrassed itself and the king with a botched assassination attempt on Hamas leader Khalid Mashaal in Amman. Mashaal, now the recognized external leader of Hamas, today operates from his sanctuary in Damascus.

Hamas escalated its violent activities in 1990 when it announced an end to its policy of attacking only Israeli soldiers and declared every Israeli both inside and outside the Green Line a legitimate target. Notably, the immediate catalyst for this change was the 1990 attack on Jerusalem's al-Aqsa mosque by Israeli extremists. The Hamas Covenant thereupon declared all of Palestine to be a Muslim administrative center, subject to special laws and edicts. Accordingly, Hamas first employed suicide bombs in 1993 in opposition to the Oslo Accords.

This violent turn corresponded with increased regional support for the organization that grew out of events surrounding the 1990–1991 Gulf War. While both Arafat and King Hussein of Jordan were making trouble for themselves by backing Iraq's invasion of Kuwait, Hamas was calling for both Saddam and the U.S.-led coalition to withdraw their forces. In response, several of the Gulf states, led by Saudi Arabia, switched their financial support for the Palestinian cause from the PLO to Hamas, bringing in revenues estimated at $28 million per month and allowing Hamas to further expand Da'wah and related activities.[4]

Arafat, now perilously close to defeat and irrelevance, saved Fatah's dominance of the Palestinian movement by embracing UN Resolution 181, accepting through its partition mandate de facto recognition of the Jewish state, and then by accepting the 1993 Oslo Accords. As part of the accords, and pursuant to an agreement signed in May 1994, Israel permitted him, as head of the Palestinian Authority, to return to Gaza and Jericho and to govern areas where Palestinians predominated. He would later brag to an astonished western diplomat that he was greater than Moses, because whereas the great biblical leader could only look at the

---

4. Ami Isseroff, "A History of the Hamas Movement," MidEastWeb.org. Available online at www.mideastweb.org/hamashistory.htm.

Promised Land from afar, he, Arafat, had personally escorted his children home.[5]

In the deal permitting Arafat's return, PA security forces were capped at nine thousand members.[6] They were permitted armaments including light personal weapons, 120 machine guns, and up to 45 wheeled armored vehicles. According to a study performed by the highly respected Strategic Assessment Initiative, "Israelis saw these forces as effectively augmenting Israel's security profile in the Occupied Territory while Palestinians saw the forces as the return of their national liberation cadre to the frontline."[7] In 1995 the number of authorized security forces was increased to thirty thousand, including eighteen thousand in the Gaza Strip, with consequent adjustments for rifles, pistols, and machine guns. Before long many of these weapons would be turned against IDF forces and civilians.

Hamas opposed UN Resolution 181 and the Oslo Accords; it was intent on continuing the struggle against Israel. This attitude kept the organization out of political activity at a time when it might have complemented its social and religious work. It did, however, occasionally lead to violent clashes with the PA. In November 1994, for instance, PA police shot and killed fourteen Palestinians who had joined a Hamas demonstration outside Gaza's Palestine mosque.

Later, following the 1995 assassination of Yitzhak Rabin and during the resulting 1996 contest between Shimon Peres and the hard-line Binyamin Netanyahu, Hamas sought to discredit the pro-Oslo Peres, employing suicide bombers to kill and maim Is-

5. Interview with senior western diplomat, July 22, 2005.

6. Strategic Assessment Initiative (SAI), "Planning Considerations for International Involvement in the Palestinian Security Sector: Overview of the Palestinian Authority Security Forces," July 2005, p. 23. Available online at www .strategicassessments.org/ontherecord/sai_publications/SAI-Planning_Consid erations_for_International_Involvement_July_2005.pdf.

7. Ibid.

raeli citizens on busy Jerusalem streets and buses. Arafat designated Muhammad Dahlan to crack down on the terrorists. Dahlan
arrested hundreds and added sacrilege to injury by shaving the
beards of many prisoners.[8] During this period, Dahlan grew close
to many in Israeli intelligence, individuals who would provide
him with information on those planning and coordinating attacks;
this made their subsequent antagonism during Intifada 2 all the
more bitter. Still, Hamas succeeded in contributing to Netanyahu's victory, not the last time Palestinian activity would doom a
Labor candidate to defeat by a rightist Likud candidate. But as
the Strategic Assessment Report noted, terrorist activity injured
very few Israelis during the 1996–99 period as the "political process and the expectation of an end to the conflict by a majority
of the public remained the most significant factors in maintaining
the unity and cohesiveness of the PA SF [Palestinian Authority
Security Force] during this period."[9]

To many Israelis, this brief period represented the high-water
mark in Arafat's good faith effort to prevent terrorism from sab-
otaging the peace process. His work in this regard was aided by
what Boaz Ganor, executive director of the International Policy
Institute for Counter-Terrorism, noted as broad agreement between Fatah and Hamas, plus Palestinian Islamic Jihad, on two
sets of short-term interests. The first encompassed the so-called
final status issues. Specifically, all parties were unified on the
need for the "withdrawal of Israel to the '67 borders, the creation
of an independent Palestinian state, the division of Jerusalem into
two capitals, and the right of return for the Palestinian refugees
to come and live within Israel in the '67 borders."[10] Though there
existed the potential for long-run tension over Israel's right to

8. "Mohammed Dahlan," Mohammed Dahlan Biography." Available online
at www.geocities.com/lawrenceoofcyberia/palbios/pa05000.html.

9. SAI, "Palestinian Authority Security Forces," p. 12.

10. Boaz Ganor, transcript of interview with author, Israel, July 26, 2005.

exist, and the future of Palestine as a secular or Islamic state, such conflicts could be finessed at the time on the basis of these parallel interests.

Ganor noted a second perception shared at the time: "Both sides agreed that the worst case scenario from the point of view of the Palestinians is a deterioration into civil war." This, he maintained, gave Arafat leverage with the extremist groups, particularly during periods when for tactical reasons he wanted a pause in terrorist activity. During those periods he might invite a Hamas leader to his office and try to persuade him that a lull was in their mutual interest. Or Arafat might threaten him with violence up to and including civil war. Overall, the process was such that he would "threaten them, persuade them, and in many cases he succeeded to limit attacks for a period of time when he wanted to. In other places he didn't use the threat and persuasion, and by that it was as if he was giving them the green light to launch terrorist attacks."[11]

Much of the rest was window-dressing or outright fraud. Weapons laboratories or storage centers would be "discovered" mysteriously on the eve of key PA meetings with the Israelis or Americans. The same occurred with the apprehension of terrorists. General Anthony Zinni, the first of the Bush administration's top military representatives to the area, during a 2002 discussion at his Williamsburg, Virginia, home, told the author the story of a 2001 visit to a Palestinian prison where a prominent terrorist suspect was supposedly under lock and key. Zinni encountered the man in the prison courtyard directing subordinates via his cell phone.

Israelis who worked with PA security forces were repeatedly frustrated, finding no inclination on their part to abort terrorist attacks before civilians were killed. Avi Dichter, who ran Shin Bet

11. Ibid.

throughout the Second Intifada, complained that the PA rarely followed up on warnings provided by Israeli intelligence of imminent terrorist attacks, except to try to find the source of the leak. "When we handed over information about attacks that are going to happen, believing arrests would take place, they took the information, and instead of looking for terrorists, they looked for the sources. We burned some sources this way, and I don't have to tell you what this means."[12]

Colonel Erez Vinner ran military intelligence on the West Bank during much of the Second Intifada. Grounded in the daily operations of Israeli counterterrorism operations, he too was distressed at the collaboration between the PA and identified terrorists. As he said, "even when we were trying and giving names and giving them places, the only thing that happened is that they were warning those terrorists that we know of them and make sure that they have to hide."[13]

Helped—or at least not harmed—by the PA, Hamas launched hundreds of terrorist operations against Israel. The political side of its operation is well coordinated, with branches in Gaza, the West Bank, and Damascus. Its intelligence arm, known as Al-Majd, spent part of its time assisting in the planning of attacks and part tracking and killing collaborators. The military wing has a cellular structure, the cells known as Izz al-Din al-Qassam squads. Journalists and others who have studied Hamas have generally been impressed by its political and operational coherence, particularly when compared to Fatah.

Early efforts to bridge the gap between Fatah and Hamas were unsuccessful. At a 1993 meeting in Khartoum, for example, Hamas offered to join the PLO only if it was awarded 40 percent of the voting delegates and if the PLO dropped its endorsement

12. Avi Dichter, notes from unrecorded interview with author, Israel, August 1, 2005.
13. Erez Vinner, transcript of interview with author, Israel, August 10, 2005.

of UN Resolution 242, which implicitly recognized Israel's right to exist. "I did not come to Sudan in order to sell you the PLO," Arafat snapped. The Hamas representative, Ibrahim Gusha, replied, "We have expressed willingness to enter the PLO and not become an alternative to it."[14] A dozen years, one Intifada, and one "earthquake" of an election later, Hamas has yet to figure out whether it belongs inside the PLO or as an Islamic alternative to it.

Beginning with the success of large-scale Israeli military operations in the spring of 2002, the PA began to evince greater interest in the negotiating track rather than letting the violence continue unabated. Yet it found Hamas in no mood to cooperate and desist in its operations. Efforts that year and the next to forge a common policy came to naught. Worse still from the perspective of the PA leadership was the fact that Hamas was collaborating with other terrorist militias, including those nominally under Fatah control.

Not that Fatah—or Arafat himself—opposed terrorist attacks against Israel. Mountains of evidence, including papers seized by the Israelis from Arafat's Moqata refuge in Ramallah, attest to his personal endorsement of terrorist operations and participation in the financing needed to keep them going. Still, there is little question that Arafat's control over units previously long-subordinate to Fatah had eroded by that point. For example, some units might well be out launching suicide bombing attacks against Israel at moments when, for tactical or strategic reasons, Arafat would have preferred a suspension of such activities. During those periods, he had little to gain from terrorist plots that served mainly to advertise his lack of control.

Hamas' eclectic partners in terror now included the Palestin-

---

14. Danny Rubinstein, "A Turning Point? The National Dialogue between Fatah and Hamas," *Strategic Assessment* 8, no. 1 (June 2005): 8–9.

ian Islamic Jihad (PIJ), Tanzim, and the al-Aqsa Martyrs Brigade. PIJ was founded by Islamic intellectuals who split off from the Palestinian Muslim Brotherhood in the early 1980s. Although Sunni, they were strongly influenced by Iran's Ayatollah Khomenni, praising him for having put the Palestinian issue at the center of regional politics and for having installed Islamic law at the center of public life. Unlike Hamas, however, PIJ seeks no elective political role and has generally been content to leave Fatah in charge of the Palestinian government. This sufferance may provide the PA with a bit of breathing room, but it also gives PIJ less of a stake in the political and diplomatic process and makes it less likely for the organization to observe any sustained period of calm, or *tahdiya*.[15]

PIJ argues that the liberation of Palestine—the jihad for Palestine—should not be framed narrowly in terms of Palestinian nationalism. Rather it is the key component of a strategy to liberate, revive, and unify the Islamic world; this constitutes the global jihad. PIJ is led from Syria and receives funding from Iran. Like Hamas, its cell-based structure makes it challenging for the Israelis to get a precise fix on its strength. Still, targeted assassinations and other raids against PIJ leaders, bomb factories, and nerve centers have both limited PIJ's operational options and advertised the quality of Israeli intelligence on the West Bank. Colonel Vinner explained how this has forced PIJ to use ad hoc methods in conducting operations.

> In Judea and Samaria this Islamic Jihad organization, this infrastructure around Jenin, has about ten regular or steady people—leaders—and the rest, they are collecting them. They go to the mosques, they find the guy who is stupid enough to commit to be the suicider—the "shahid." They find somebody else

15. Ibid. See also SAI, "Palestinian Authority Security Forces," p. 43.

who will help them to pass the checkpoints, and they build an operation.[16]

Tanzim, another armed faction, flowered briefly as a Palestinian youth organization during the First Intifada. It was reconstituted by Arafat's Fatah party in the mid-1990s as a mechanism for containing militant and fundamentalist opposition to the political, security, and economic regime implemented during the period of the Oslo Accords (1993–2001). Tanzim recruits were used in considerable numbers by Arafat as members of his Security Forces and the elite Force 17, two of the many militias Arafat maintained to do his bidding while keeping the security apparatus divided and unthreatening.

Tanzim's most illustrious leader was Marwan Barghouti, an alumnus of Israeli jails who taught himself flawless Hebrew while imprisoned and emerged to become a key early player in the triangular security consultations involving Israel, the PA, and the United States. He also became head of Fatah's Supreme Council on the West Bank, leading many Israeli observers to see him as a likely successor to Arafat. Many relished this prospect.

As Arafat moved to armed conflict, however, and emptied his jails of hundreds of Hamas and PIJ prisoners in the process, Tanzim dutifully switched to terrorism. Its specialties were drive-by shootings and, later, suicide bombings. Barghouti, still considered a pragmatic moderate in some Israeli circles, was the object of a failed Israeli assassination attempt in 2001.[17] Captured in April the following year, tried in civilian court, and convicted of five murder counts, he was sentenced to five life terms plus forty years for other violent activity even as he was acquitted of thirty-three

---

16. Interview with Vinner.

17. Clyde Haberman, "Israeli Missiles Miss Leader of Convoy; Aide Injured," *New York Times*, August 5, 2001.

other murders.[18] While shunning a complete defense at his trial, he did seek to rebut charges of terrorism, offering: "I am not a terrorist, but neither am I a pacifist. I am simply a regular guy from the Palestinian street advocating only what every other oppressed person has advocated—the right to help myself in the absence of help from anywhere else."[19]

The al-Aqsa Brigades, like Tanzim, emerged during the Second Intifada. In its September 2005 analysis of the Palestinian security sector, SAI described the Brigades not as a single organization, but as "loosely aggregated localized groups who were established at the beginning of the Second Intifada with informal Fatah support to undertake resistance activity against Israel."

Founded by a core of radicals from the Balata refugee camp on the West Bank, the al-Aqsa Brigades received much of their early political direction and material support from Tanzim. As offshoots of Fatah, both groups were at first regarded both by Israelis and Palestinians as moderates, as both echoed Fatah's call for a two-state solution. Yet as they warmed to the fight, some began invoking Islamic motifs, making Islam versus Judaism a central tenet of the Second Intifada. Their underlying claim was that the Oslo years proved the Israelis had no intention of withdrawing from the occupation of Palestinian territories and that Israel only understands violence. Leaders of the al-Aqsa Brigades accordingly contend that Israel should be wiped off the map and that Palestinian refugees should all be permitted to return to their former homes.

The Brigades and Tanzim have taken responsibility for three hundred terrorist attacks in which Israeli civilians were killed. Israeli officials maintain that since the Second Intifada erupted in

18. United Press International, "Israeli Court Sentences Palestinian Leader," *UPI*, June 6, 2004.

19. Marwan Barghouti, "Want Security? End the Occupation," *Washington Post*, January 15, 2002.

2000, the two groups have carried out or attempted more than fifteen hundred separate attacks, including suicide bombings, car bombings, shootings, kidnappings, and knife attacks. Some of these occurred in concert with Hamas and/or PIJ while others constituted organic affairs.[20]

Whatever the result of these individual encounters, the PA and its own security forces were the big losers. When directly involved in the fighting they were targeted by IDF forces for retaliation. And as SAI reported:

> When other organizations—Hamas, PIJ, Tanzim or the Al-Aqsa Martyrs Brigades—initiated the actions, the Israeli government then embarked on a new policy of targeting official Palestinian institutions in the hope that this would encourage the PA SF [Palestinian Authority Security Forces] to take a more active role in quelling the increasing violence.[21]

This proved fortuitous for the other groups and particularly so for Hamas, which sought to eventually supplant Fatah as the leader of the Palestinian cause. For Hamas, the situation was such that "by increasing attacks against Israel, they could effectively dismantle the apparatus of their chief rival while placing all the blame on Israel."[22]

Chief PA negotiator Saeb Erakat later complained that the Israeli attacks against the PA SF left the field open to Hamas. "They did not create the militias," he declared, "but the militias in the absence of Palestinian security forces grew naturally. . . . All you need are guns, five or six people, and you can impose your law in the street and at that corner. And that's the story in Nablus, that's the story in Jenin, that's the story in Gaza."[23]

20. Yael Shahar, "The al-Aqsa Martyrs Brigades," Institute for Counter-Terrorism, March 24, 2002. Available online at www.ict.org.il/articles/articledet .cfm?articleid=430.

21. SAI, "Palestinian Authority Security Forces," p. 13.

22. Ibid.

23. Saeb Erakat, transcript of interview with author, Jericho, August 6, 2005.

At any point in time, the objectives of each group may militate against any particular actor initiating violence. During the periods immediately preceding and following the Gaza pullout, for example, the PA needed Israel's help on a host of "day after" issues, including access to Israel and the West Bank and economic development. An even greater concern involved the possibility that Israel would conclude the PA was hopelessly ineffective and adopt a far more onerous "disengagement" plan on the West Bank that would close some settlements while preserving a large Israeli security presence on the ground. To preempt that result, the PA had to show it could enforce the agreed-upon period of quiet not only through the Gaza pullout but months beyond that.

The other groups had reasons of their own to comply with the period of calm. Tanzim and the Brigades did not wish to bring the wrath of the Israelis on their heads. Hamas, on the other hand, needed to use the pullout to drive home its message that armed resistance works. Having also decided to compete in the political arena, it had to show that it could control its forces so as not to invite an unwanted Israeli response. PIJ, meanwhile, although pressed hard by Israel, could use a period of relative quietude to lick its West Bank wounds and start rebuilding its capabilities.

The bottom line is that nearly every affected Palestinian faction considered itself better off with the Israelis gone from Gaza than with their staying. Hamas still tried to reinforce its narrative of Israelis retreating in the face of armed resistance by firing some rockets in early July. Instead, it brought upon itself an angry response from the broader Palestinian populace.[24] Ahmad Abd Alrahman explained that when the pullout was first announced many Palestinians saw it as a trick. "But when they looked to the

24. Deutsche Presse-Agentur, "Analysis: PA and Hamas in Power Struggle; Ceasefire in Danger," July 15, 2005; and Steven Gutkin, "Hamas, Ruling Fatah Agree to End Clashes after Tense Week," *Associated Press*, July 19, 2005.

Israelis taking their installations from the settlements, they began to believe that this disengagement means withdrawal, so they began to support the Authority, you see, and to tell Hamas and others, 'Why are you hitting these stupid rockets? Why? The Israelis are leaving. What are you doing?'"[25]

When we met in his Ramallah office, Hassan Yousef, Hamas' leader in the West Bank, said the rocket attack that bothered Alrahman was in retaliation for several Israeli provocations, including two targeted assassination attempts and the killing of two Hamas members in the Balata refugee camp. But he left no doubt his organization was taking the tahdiya seriously. "We want Israel to withdraw from our lands," he said, "and we are with this step. And we will not put any problem in front of their withdrawing. There will not be any shooting from our side during that disengagement."[26]

Beyond the Gaza disengagement, Hamas was waiting to see what Sharon would do on the remainder of the West Bank. Hamas was participating on the political track and needed a period of reduced tensions to organize its political machine. When Hassan suggested to the author that he would welcome a private unreported meeting with the U.S. ambassador, he sounded a bit grandiose but not illogical. Engagement with the United States at that time was much in Hamas' interest. For one thing, the organization did not want the United States to press Abu Mazen to further delay the elections. Also, without active behind-the-scenes activity by Washington, Israel could use Hamas' involvement to delegitimize the elections while remaining aloof from negotiations. Hence, Hamas wanted negotiations as a political tool to dramatize its role as a defender of *both* Palestinian interests and

25. Ahmad Abd Alrahman, transcript of interview with author, Ramallah, July 29, 2005.

26. Hassan Yousef, transcript of interview with author, Ramallah, July 28, 2005.

Islamic values but without the prospect of a treaty arranging an end to the violence.

Hamas, therefore, sought at least informal recognition by the United States not as a menacing terrorist clan but rather as a maturing political organization. "Yes," said Yousef, "So we are not like other movements such as the Fatah movement. We are one movement and to deal with a movement with one leader is much better than to deal with a movement with many leaders." It is, of course, one thing to seek quiet contacts as an "out" and something else to consider how to relate to those same nations as the elected government of a quasi state, the problem Hamas is now confronting.

Before its election, Hamas did not conceal the fact that it is merely biding its time for a renewal of the armed struggle against Israel. When the author asked Sami Abu Zuhri, chief spokesman for Hamas in Gaza, whether the Second Intifada was a military failure, he rejected the notion. Instead, he viewed it as vindication for the armed struggle: "First," he offered, "there is no freedom without paying a price. Secondly, we are witnessing the result of such resistance through the withdrawal from the Gaza Strip, because this withdrawal is not a gift to the Palestinian people, but is an official escape from the Gaza Strip."[27]

By endorsing the Road Map, the PA committed itself to dismantling the apparatus of terrorism. Abu Mazen issued a call for independent militias to merge with government security forces but the plan was summarily rejected by Hamas and the others. The PA did not press the issue. According to SAI, it was in no condition to do so. The following are excerpts from its seventy-eight-page report, "Planning Considerations for International Involvement in the Palestinian Security Sector," as noted above:

27. Sami Abu Zuhri, transcript of interview with author, Gaza, July 30, 2005.

- "There is considerable overlap in purpose and functional capacity within the PA SF. This is partly a legacy of Yasser Arafat's fear of any one Service Commander becoming too powerful and thus presenting a challenge to his own authority."

- "Several forces, particularly those which were created by Yasser Arafat to counter-balance perceived challengers, are not currently part of any clear chain of command."

- "One of the most damaging aspects of the years of the Second Intifada has been the divergence of security organizations on the Gaza Strip and the West Bank."

- "Training capacity was severely eroded as a result of Israel's destruction of Palestinian training facilities. Training resources are inadequate, and live firing practice is constrained by a lack of arms and munitions."

- "All forces, but in particular the Civil Police and NSF [National Security Force], suffer from a degree of low self-esteem and public status as a result of years of being unable to protect the civilian population against IF [Israeli Forces] incursions, IF's demonstrated ability to damage PA SF forces at will, and openly degrading treatment by Israeli soldiers in plain view of civilians."

- "There is little standardization of vehicle types even among the same units. There is a shortage of 4-wheel-drive vehicles capable of negotiating the local terrain, particularly in the West Bank."

- "Lack of repair and replacements, theft, Israeli military initiatives during the second Intifada and a lack of maintenance have left arms stocks depleted and dilapidated. . . . Ammunition is in very short supply and much of what is available is in poor condition and unreliable. The current ratio of personnel to weapons is 4:1. Meanwhile, non-state factions are, by contrast, relatively well-armed."[28]

Ironically in light of later events, it was the Israelis who facilitated the acquisition of small arms by the PA. Thus, every Israeli gunshot death and injury seemed to become a political issue after the Oslo process devolved into the Second Intifada. This time around, when the PA sought permission to bring weapons and military vehicles into the country, the Israelis said no to both lethal weapons and armored equipment. The reaction from Palestinians like Saeb Erakat was bitter:

> I need bullets. If I'm attacked by militias, I cannot fight them with a speech. I cannot. Or a sermon. And the Israelis are saying no, we cannot allow you to have bullets. . . . They are tying my hands, they are tying my legs, they are throwing me into the ocean. "Hey Congress, look at them! They're not swimming! They are no partner! They're not doing anything! They're drowning! What good are they to me?"[29]

Many Israelis argue that Abu Mazen doth protest too much. Avi Dichter said the PA should have begun to move against Hamas on the West Bank where, in his estimate, four years of sweeps, arrests, home demolitions, targeted assassinations, and related counterterrorism efforts left Hamas with a minimally functional base of operations in the territory. This analysis was confirmed in a recent study of Hamas conducted by the generally pro-Palestinian *Middle East Report*. As the study concluded, toward the end of Israeli counterterrorism operations, "sound intelligence, helicopter gunships and death squads proved thorough at wiping out what remained of Hamas' West Bank military cadre."[30]

28. SAI, "Palestinian Authority Security Forces," supra.
29. Interview with Erakat.
30. Graham Usher, "The New Hamas: Between Resistance and Participation,"

In Gaza, by contrast, Israel tried less and accomplished less. Yes, Israel conducted targeted assassinations of Gaza-based Hamas leaders, including Ismail Abu Shanab, Sheikh Achmad Yassin, Ibrihim Maqadmeh, and Abd al-Aziz Rantisi. Most of its Gaza military actions, however, were in response to terrorist attacks on Israeli settlers. In other words, Israel undertook only limited measures to undermine the long-term capabilities of terrorist groups *before* attacks occurred. As a result, terrorist militias continued to thrive in Gaza, becoming even larger and better armed after the pullout.

During the August 2003 cease-fire following the appointment of Abu Mazen as prime minister, a suicide bomber linked to Hamas detonated a bomb aboard a bus in Jerusalem.[31] Although leaders of the organization condemned the attack, and some analysts insisted the perpetrators were a rump group based in Hebron, the international reaction was devastating. Within days, the PA, Britain, and the United States froze the bank accounts of Islamic charities within their respective jurisdictions. Funding from most countries besides Iran all but dried up. And in September, the European Union put the entire organization—not just its military wing—on its terrorism blacklist.[32]

Some experienced analysts argue that such moves to undermine Hamas come at the precise moment when it seeks to change its terrorist ways and move in the direction of conventional politics. By this logic, it seeks reform and good government, propor-

---

Middle East Report, August 21, 2005. Available online at www.merip.org/mero/mero082105.html.

31. Peter Mackler, "20 Dead, More Than 100 Injured in Massive Jerusalem Bus Blast," *Agence France Presse–English*, August 19, 2003.

32. See, for example, "Palestinian PM Condemns 'Terrible' Bus Bombing, Calls Off Hamas Talks," *Agence France Presse–English*, August 20, 2003; "Britain's Foreign Secretary Condemns Jerusalem Bomb Blast," *Agence France Presse–English*, August 20, 2003; and "Bush Freezes Assets of Hamas Leaders," *Economic Times*, August 24, 2003.

tional representation and an end to corruption. Moreover, according to these analysts, its desire for a window to Washington is probably sincere. Hamas, according to Sheikh Ahmad Hajj, a member of the organization's governing Shura Council, is willing to go even further:

> We would negotiate with Israel since that is the power that usurped our rights. If negotiations fail, we will call on the world to intervene. If this fails, we will go back to resistance. But if Israel were to agree with our internationally recognized rights—including the refugees' right of return—the Shura Council would seriously consider recognizing Israel in the interests of world peace.[33]

While the statement has more caveats than a prescription drug advertisement, the change in tone, particularly when viewed in conjunction with its embrace of the March 2005 Cairo Declaration and the decision to participate in elective Palestinian politics could be significant. Of course, the history of the "right of return" fouling negotiations begs for caution, as does the organization's genocidal charter and its stated commitment to a single Islamic state.

Before the outbreak of the Second Intifada, Hamas consistently captured about 17 percent in "beauty contest" polls against Fatah. That percentage doubled during the period of fighting. At a Gaza rally in 2002 marking the fifteenth anniversary of the organization, forty thousand heard Shiekh Yassin predict the demise of Israel within twenty-five years. The organization had also developed a political agenda. Its three main items were electoral reform, including proportional representation, the conduct of elections for the Palestinian Legislative Council, and the restructuring of the PLO to guaranty Hamas 40 percent of the elected positions.

33. Usher, "New Hamas."

In local elections held in December 2004 and January and May 2005, Hamas won a majority of all contested seats plus separate majorities in 30 percent of all councils. It scored its most stunning victories in Bethlehem and Qalqilya, the latter surrounded by the new Israeli security fence. The upsets led Abu Mazen to postpone legislative council elections initially scheduled for July 2005 until January 2006 in the hope that economic benefits from the Israeli Gaza withdrawal would bring the voters back to Fatah by the new date. Unfortunately for Fatah, pervasive criminal and political violence and the failure of many "day after" benefits to reach the people of Gaza did not help Abu Mazen's case. Strong Hamas showings in local November balloting, including outright wins in both Nablus and Jenin, called Fatah's move into question. The tremors, largely discounted as local responses to local issues, were in fact rumblings of the great January earthquake to come; this topic will be analyzed in detail in chapter 7.

In Qalqilya, the Hamas municipal victory was followed by edicts canceling a scheduled dance and concert as well as the consideration of other measures to make the town more "Islamic." To Palestinian liberals, the notion of an Islamic fundamentalist state on Palestinian soil in the vein of Saudi Arabia or Iran is almost unbearable. Hanan Ashwari, running for the legislature as a reform "Third Way" party candidate, blamed the PA for part of the problem in that it ignored nation-building and institution building, the rule of law, and respect for human rights. She worried that the power struggle in Gaza among militias operating outside government control might lead to internal disintegration. And she predicted that the longer the conflict with Israel remains unresolved the more likely it is that one form of tyranny will replace another; as she concluded:

> So we're seeing in this something more important than just a
> political process—we're seeing a struggle over the soul of Pal-

estine. What kind of system are we going to have? What kind
of a society? A society that prevents festivals and music and
creativity, and separates the sexes, and coerces people into
strong closed systems—or a society that's open, democratic, plu-
ralistic, tolerant. To me this is important.[34]

Ms. Ashwari won her seat only to find that it gave her a ring-
side view of the new Hamas-dominated legislature.

34. Hanan Ashwari, transcript of interview with author, Jerusalem, July 29,
2005.

6. The Settlements

RON NACHMAN WINCED and his lips emitted an audible grunt of pain as he pushed himself from his car to stand erect on the road that traces the settlement of Ariel. Ariel is one of three West Bank settlements that are also cities, a source of considerable pride to Nachman, who founded the place twenty-seven years ago and now serves as mayor. He has been losing bone at the base of his spine for several years and is now rarely free of acute distress. Yet he is a proud, combative man who does not dwell on the bad cards he has been dealt, but rather on how he has played his hand. He provided a taste of his gruff personality by delivering a long, plaintive lecture to one visitor who had referred to him as a "settler."

"Let the Arabs call us settlers," he declared. "I'm a fourth-generation Jewish Palestinian. My great-grandfather came here in the first *Aliyah*. That was 1885. My family has never left. This is our land.[1]

"You've already seen what we started with here," he continued, referring to photographs of a single caravan resting on a pile of rocks. "Well this here is the first row of houses I put up, right along the ridge line." He paused long enough to allow his listeners to get a fix on Palestinian villages visible from the ridge. "I wanted the Arabs in those villages down there to see us every

---

1. Ron Nachman, notes of interview with author, Ariel, approx. August 9, 2005.

time they came out of their doors. I wanted them to know we are here. I wanted them to know we weren't going anywhere."[2]

The Arabs have ample reason to know that Ariel is there. It runs for 3.1 miles along a ridge line that begins at an altitude of over 1,800 feet and climbs another 400 feet. The town has its share of needed and ongoing changes. Still to be repaired, for example, is a gymnasium roof that caved in years ago during a mighty snow storm; Nachman claims a freeze on settlement construction imposed during the premiership of Yitzhak Rabin is to blame. Several hundred yards away a bulldozer was preparing the ground for construction of a temporary fence to protect the settlement from Palestinian infiltration. The Sharon government had announced months earlier that the West Bank security wall would protect Ariel, its bloc of at least fourteen settlements, and some thirty-seven thousand settlers, but quiet U.S. pressure caused Sharon to postpone the link. At least seven illegal outposts also reside within the Ariel bloc. Their apparent purpose is to further isolate the Palestinian villages while providing the Israeli settlements in the area with greater contiguity.

The large Palestinian town of Salfit sits to the south of Ariel; to the north are several smaller Arab villages. Modern highways— Route 60 runs north-south while Route 5 runs east-west—serve the settlements but have been closed to Palestinian motorists during most of the period since the Second Intifada began. When our car with three passengers turned from Ariel in the direction of Jerusalem, IDF troops at a guard post urged us to turn back because of sniper fire along the road. We did.

The visitor is soon lost in a haze of road numbers amid the names of Jewish settlements and Palestinian villages. Even so, what is strikingly clear is that the infrastructure developed over the years was put in place to suit what an old administrative law

2. Ibid.

practitioner in the United States might have termed the "public convenience and necessity" of the settlers and not the Palestinians. It is the latter's villages that have lost contiguity because of the roads and settlement boundaries, their farmlands that wound up on the wrong side of a road or fence, their commuting time from village to village that has doubled or trebled, their access to schools, hospitals, jobs, and former neighbors that has been made infinitely more challenging.

"We're not trying to make life tough for them," Nachman insisted. "See down there. That's a tunnel we've built that goes from the village to the agricultural land. That solves one problem. We're trying to live with them, not drive them out." He speaks haltingly of the kind of political solution he envisions. Maybe a few slivers of land on the West Bank could go to the Arabs. Politically, however, those people should be participating in the Palestinian state that has become Jordan. After all, Jordan already has a Palestinian majority. And clearly they are not Israelis. Demography? Not an issue. National identity is all that counts.

Nachman is far from the only Israeli to urge the involvement of neighboring Arab states in solving the Israeli-Palestinian conflict. Israel Harel, a reflective *Haaretz* columnist, believes the Palestinians keep trying to eliminate Israel because they know that even 5,500 square kilometers—all of Gaza and the West Bank— is insufficient for the large, rapidly growing Palestinian population. The key to his solution is thus to convince Egypt to donate about thirty thousand square kilometers of the now barren Sinai which the Palestinians could live on, farm, and own.[3] The proposal reminds one of the tale of a Jewish village in tsarist Russia that debated whether it would be a good or bad thing for one of the eligible village girls to wed the tsar's son. After hours of back-

---

3. Israel Harel, "Preserve The Land," in *Israel and the Palestinians: Israeli Policy Options*, ed. Mark Heller and Rosemary Hollis (London: Chatham House, 2005), p. 47.

and-forth the shared conclusion was that the step would be beneficial. "Wonderful," declared the local wise man, "now all we have to do is convince the tsar."

The Labor government that presided over the colossal victory in the 1967 Six Days' War explored "land for peace" options with its defeated neighbors during the period that followed but never concluded a deal. Partly this was due to the collective Arab mindset at the time, best illustrated by the famous "Three No's" resolution adopted by the Arab League Summit in Khartoum that September: "no negotiations, no recognition of Israel, and no peace with the Zionist entity."[4] At the very least, regional political conditions were not conducive to a land for peace arrangement.

Nor did the international scene improve matters. On November 22 of the same year, the UN Security Council passed Resolution 242, calling on Israel to withdraw from "territories occupied" during the war. This is a formulation that, in the context of the Palestinian-Israeli and Arab-Israeli land debates and related provisions declaring the right of states in the region to "secure and recognized boundaries," cannot be interpreted as requiring either a total or an immediate Israeli pullout. Although coming amid a now-defunct cold war superpower rivalry for influence in the Middle East, this international development has borne upon the status of the Occupied Territories through to the present.

At the time of the 1967 victory, the Israeli government had no immediate interest in settlements. Rather, Defense Minister Moshe Dayan believed in self-government for the Occupied Territories, assuming the interim period of occupation would be followed by a negotiated end to the conflict. Dayan deferred to the Jordanians in matters of social and political concern to the Palestinians. The Jordanian dinar was the local currency, local Jordanian law remained in place, and a revised Jordanian curricu-

4. Ibid, p. 39.

lum was taught in the schools. While over time the economic relationship between Israel and the territories took on more than a faintly colonialist hue, at the outset the relationship seemed to reflect mutual interest. Soon Palestinians were providing one-quarter of Israel's factory labor and one-half of its construction and service labor. The territories became important markets for Israeli goods. The Labor government introduced mechanized agriculture to places where none had previously existed, brought television to the territories, and initiated educational and health care improvements that had strong quality-of-life components. Between 1968 and 1973, the GNP of the territories grew at a stunning annual rate of 14.5 percent.[5]

The government had no immediate intention of building settlements in the Occupied Territories, but some of its citizens did. The breakthrough came at a place named Kfar Etzion, a place just east of Jerusalem abutting today's Green Line. In 1927, a group of ultra-orthodox Jews from Jerusalem and a handful of recently arrived Yemenites founded the settlement, calling it Migdal Eder. It was destroyed by rioting Arabs two years later. A few years afterward, the site was purchased by a man named Shmuel Yosef Holtzman, who named it Kfar Etzion in his own honor. This settlement lasted only until the outbreak of the 1936 Arab uprising, when its residents fled and its structures were demolished. Jews again returned to build four communities during the 1943–47 period, but they fell to the Jordanian Army in the 1948 war; little if anything was left standing. Fifteen captured Jewish fighters were machine-gunned by the Jordanians. Because of that atrocity many of today's settlers believe they live on hallowed land, drenched as it is with Jewish blood.[6]

5. United States Library of Congress, *Country Studies: Israel*, "The Occupied Territories." Available online at http://countrystudies.us/israel/.

6. Dror Etkes and Lara Friedman, "Gush Etzion," *Settlements in Focus*, Peace Now/Americans for Peace Now, November 2005, p. 1.

After Israel recaptured the area in 1967, a number of Israelis—including descendants of those who fell fighting the 1948 battle for the settlement—asked the government for permission to resettle the area. Jerusalem refused but the settlers moved on their own. Before long, the government found itself defending them against Palestinian attacks and providing the full range of social and educational services to make the settlements viable.

A second case of such "adverse possession" involved the biblical city of Hebron, where Abraham and his family are believed by many Jews, Muslims, and Christians to be buried. Jews had lived in Hebron over the centuries, even when the territory was under the control of other actors. In 1929, frenzied anti-Jewish Arab mobs brutally murdered sixty-seven Jewish residents of the city even as more than four hundred others were given refuge by Arab neighbors. The survivors soon left Hebron.[7]

In 1968, extremist Rabbi Moshe Levinger organized a movement to resettle all parts of biblical Israel beginning with its most ancient city. He and his followers advertised for fellow Jews who wanted to spend Passover in Hebron and wound up with eighty-eight celebrants at the city's Park Hotel. Days later, Levinger announced his intention to stay in Hebron. Dayan proposed instead that the settlers move to a military base overlooking the city. Such was the founding of the Kiryat Arba settlement.

In 1978, a group of ten women and forty children moved in the dead of night from Kiryat Arba to a medical clinic, Beit Hadassah, which had been abandoned since the 1929 riots. By that time, Menachem Begin and his Likud Party were in power in Israel and while he favored settlement of the entire land of Israel, he was wary of putting Jews in the heart of Arab communities. While Begin's first inclination was to starve the Jewish residents out, he eventually settled for permitting them to come and go

---

7. Lara Friedman and Dror Etkes, "Hebron," *Settlements in Focus*, Peace Now/Americans for Peace Now, October 2005, p. 2.

from Beit Hadassah but to restrict anyone else from entering the building.[8]

On Friday nights, some Kiryat Arba residents, including Yeshiva students, would attend nearby services with the women and children of Beit Hadassah. When the women and children returned to Beit Hadassah, the men and older boys would dance to the building and say prayers over the Sabbath wine for them. In early May 1980, Arab terrorists positioned on a roof across the street from Beit Hadassah attacked the celebrants with guns and grenades, killing six of them and wounding twenty. Begin responded by officially authorizing the establishment of a Jewish community protected by IDF in the heart of Hebron.[9]

That community, along with Kiryat Arba, understandably attracts some of the most virulently anti-Arab Israelis in the entire West Bank, Israelis who in many cases would like to be employed pushing Palestinians back across the Jordan River. The relationship of many of the settlers with the local IDF forces keeping the parties apart is strained; incidents of violence are common. Private Israeli citizens are discouraged from driving their own vehicles to Hebron. Buses serving the city sport bullet-proof windows in an effort to frustrate snipers. On February 25, 1994, Dr. Baruch Goldstein, a Brooklyn-born settler, entered the Ibrahimi Mosque—the Muslim portion of the Tomb of the Patriarchs—and opened fire with his M-16 rifle, killing twenty-nine Arab worshippers and wounding hundreds more before he was killed by surviving worshippers. He was buried at Kiryat Arba, a hero to his fellow Jewish fanatics. A plaque marking his grave salutes him as "a righteous and holy man . . . who devoted his soul to the Jews, Jewish religion and Jewish land. His hands are innocent and his heart is pure."[10]

The early post-1967 Labor governments lacked a desire to

8. Ibid, p. 2.
9. Ibid, p. 3.
10. Ibid, p. 3.

populate biblical Israel with settlers. Most of its leadership, however, had grown up during the pre-statehood Kibbutz Era when
tiny outposts offered protection against small-scale raids and
provocations, reinforcing the brand of communalism that was a
central ethic of the emerging state. For that reason, they listened
closely in 1968 when Deputy Prime Minister Yigal Allon proposed
a series of settlements along the Jordan Valley and eastern slopes
of the mountain ridges that run inland from the Sea of Galilee to
the Dead Sea. The area in question, he argued, was critical to
Israel's ability to defend itself against attack from Jordan or Iraq.
It could be buttressed by a series of purely military outposts (*Na-
hals*). Due to the oppressively hot climate and marginal agricultural productivity of the area, the local Palestinian population was
small so that displacement, perhaps resulting in increased antagonism, could be limited. Accordingly, the "Allon Plan" envisioned
future Israeli annexation of the area.[11]

Today there are twenty-seven Eastern Strip–Jordan Valley settlements and five military outposts with a total of just under nine
thousand settlers, but there has been no new construction since
the mid-1980s.[12] At one point the Sharon-Olmert government announced its intention to build an "eastern fence" to protect these
settlements but deferred to international pressure and has still to
begin the project. The organization Peace Now, which tracks settlement activity, recently reported an effort by Minister of Agriculture Yisrael Katz, in conjunction with the World Zionist Organization's Settlement Department, to earmark $32 million in
incentives and other subsidies to attract additional numbers of
Israelis to these settlements.[13] Yet during the 2000 Camp David

11. See "The Allon Plan," MidEastWeb.org. Available online at www
.mideastweb.org/alonplan.htm.
12. Lara Friedman and Dror Etkes, "Eastern Strip of the West Bank," *Settlements in Focus*, Peace Now/Americans for Peace Now, September 2005, p. 1.
13. Ibid, p.3.

negotiations, Ehud Barak's negotiators agreed to yield the area to Palestinian sovereignty. Apparently, the establishment of diplomatic relations with Jordan and the removal of the Saddam Hussein regime in Iraq greatly diminish the national security value of these settlements even if Alon had a point thirty-five years earlier. In describing his own plans for the West Bank today, Prime Minister Olmert has described the Jordan Valley as Israel's "security border," an imprecise term that, if expansively applied, could add 15 to 35 percent to the West Bank land Israel might seek to appropriate.

Ariel, on the other hand, was precisely the kind of project that marked the difference in ideology between Labor and the Likud a generation ago. Where Labor used settlements to reinforce claims to the Jerusalem area and defend the country against attack from the east, Likud wanted to settle all of biblical Israel. The 1977 election, in which the Likud fused together a coalition of Greater Israel advocates, Jews of Middle Eastern heritage, and those who had never bought into Labor's idealistic socialism, marked an early turning point in the settler movement. Backed by unapologetic expansionist movements like Gush Emunim (Bloc of the Faithful) and resourceful Likud ministers like Ariel Sharon, Israel placed settlements in strategic places, gave them room to grow, and reinforced their presence by putting other settlements nearby, all part of a strategy to make it hard if not impossible for Palestinian villages to expand or to gain the territorial cohesion necessary to form a state. Small at the start, as was typical of most such settlements, Ariel had plenty of elbow room in which to expand. More important, it was smack in the heart of the West Bank. Located ten miles from the closest Green Line point, twenty-five miles from Tel Aviv, and thirty from Jerusalem, it announced to the Palestinians that every part of their land was open to Israeli settlement. Unlike other big blocs such as Gush Emunim and Ma'aleh Adumim, it could not be conceptualized as integral to Jerusalem or Tel Aviv. And unlike most of the other settlements far from the Green Line, it was and remains overwhelmingly secular.

"We've got nearly twenty thousand people now," Ron Nachman was saying. "Just over half of them [are] Russian. And we're a city—hotel, university, even an electron accelerator, one of only nine in the whole country. Not bad for a pile of rocks and a caravan."[14] He failed to mention the municipal court and police station that add to the city's development and sense of permanence.

Amid fears raised by his embrace of unilateral disengagement, Sharon visited Ariel in July 2005 and told residents exactly what Nachman wanted them to hear. "I want to make it clear," he emphasized, "that this bloc will always remain a part of Israel and there will always be territorial contiguity between the Ariel bloc and the rest of Israel."[15] Yet this may be an easier policy to declare than to achieve, particularly if a current or future Israeli prime minister believes he could establish the final Israeli borders through negotiation as opposed to unilateral action. Ehud Barak recalled that at Camp David, he too insisted on retaining Ariel with the support of President Clinton and observing: "Look, I don't know what will happen. In the past, for me it's not a hypothesis—I was there and I was ready to go further than any other Israeli leader, and Ariel was inside the line that was proposed by us to the Palestinians and backed at Camp David by Clinton. It included Ariel."[16]

At Camp David, Palestinian representatives rejected the plan. They were clearly concerned about "cantonization," winding up with pockets of land isolated by Israeli settlements, roads, and restrictive travel arrangements and affecting hundreds of

14. Interview with Nachman.
15. "Ariel—Israel's Smart City," *Surprisingly Engaging*, Ariel Municipality & Ariel Development Fund, July 21, 2005.
16. Ehud Barak, transcript of interview with author, Israel, August 17, 2005.

thousands of Palestinians. The issue was finessed in the Clinton Parameters which, according to a Peace Now paper, simply listed relevant goals in dealing with the settlements issue including retaining 80 percent of settlers in existing blocs, ensuring Palestinian territorial contiguity, minimizing areas annexed to Israel, and limiting the number of Palestinians affected.[17] Taking the Parameters a step further, the Virtual Geneva Accord would consider Ariel as Palestinian territory at least until the parties themselves negotiate contrary arrangements.[18] An Israeli source familiar with the period of negotiations that began with Camp David and ended at Taba states that at Taba the Palestinians indicated a willingness to permit Ariel, but not the other settlements and outposts in its bloc, to remain Israeli, all in the framework of land swaps, with some land now part of Israel to go to the Palestinians.

As the blocs have grown, complicating issues have developed. Gush Etzion, for example existed for most of its development as a growing suburb of Jerusalem catering mostly to orthodox and ultra-orthodox residents. These people are settlers only in the technical sense of the word. Their communities are so integral to the Jerusalem area that not even the Palestinians talk seriously about the bloc's separation from Israel at the conclusion of final status negotiations. But one of its newer and fastest growing settlements, Efrat, strays far from the Green Line, running nearly to Bethlehem and thereby restricting the orderly development of affected Palestinian communities. Efrat's leader is Rabbi Shlomo Riskin, who grew up in the Bedford-Stuyvesant area of Brooklyn and for many years presided over the large congregation at Lincoln Center in Manhattan. He speaks proudly of the good relations his community maintains with neighboring Palestinian vil-

17. Dror Etkes and Lara Friedman, "Ariel and Ariel Bloc," *Settlements in Focus*, Peace Now/Americans for Peace Now, May 2005, p. 3.

18. The Geneva Accord, "Draft Permanent Status Agreement," as published by *Haaretz*, October 2003. Available online at www.haaretz.com/hasen/pages/ShArt.jhtml?itemNo=351461.

lagers, about eighteen thousand of whom now reside inside the declared borders of Gush Etzion but outside the Green Line.

"Number one, I would like very much to see a Palestinian state," he said. "I think it's important for the Palestinians."[19] Yet Riskin opposed Sharon's unilateral disengagement plan, claiming it rewarded terrorism. And he was unpleasantly surprised when the Virtual Geneva Accord failed to include Efrat on the Israeli side of the adjusted border. "But some people from the Geneva Accord say they made a mistake by not putting it in," he noted. "If they had it to do over they would put it in because to break us up from Gush Etzion makes no sense."[20]

Throughout Israel, the West Bank, and Gaza, the political situation is in some turmoil and negotiations are on hold—a situation the Hamas victory in January's legislative races and the results of Israeli elections in March 2006 may do more to muddy than clarify. Still, the facts on the ground do change and bring potentially long-lasting effects. Take, for example, the E-1 project planned by Israel, which is prominent among the litany of Palestinian concerns. To many Israelis, the plan to build a new neighborhood northeast of Jerusalem and west of the Ma'ale Adumim settlement is a logical addition to a stretch of land that may be comfortably categorized as a suburb of Jerusalem and thus, in the Israeli mind, falls outside the mandate of UN Resolution 242 and its post-1973 cousin, Resolution 338. The Israeli anti-settlement community, however, offers a far graver prognosis. As reported by Peace Now:

> Construction of E-1 would jeopardize the hopes for a two-state solution. It would, by design, block off the narrow undeveloped land corridor which runs east of Jerusalem and which is necessary for any meaningful future connection between the south-

19. Rabbi Shlomo Riskin, transcript of interview with author, Israel, August 7, 2005.
20. Ibid.

ern and northern parts of the West Bank. It would thus break
the West Bank into two parts—north and south. It would also
sever access to East Jerusalem for Palestinians in the West bank,
and sever access to the West Bank for Palestinian residents of
East Jerusalem.[21]

As noted earlier, the E-1 controversy does not lend itself to
easy compromise. Developed under the Israeli plan, it blocks Palestinian north-south contiguity. In Palestinian hands, it impedes
east-west Israeli contiguity.

Meanwhile, the Palestinians take issue with techniques employed by the Israelis to stake out their positions on the West
Bank. One is the series of by-pass roads constructed throughout
Area C, the 60 percent of the West Bank where, under the Oslo
Accords, Israel remained responsible for both security and civil
administration until a permanent status agreement is reached.
The roads permit Israelis to (1) travel to and from or between
settlements while avoiding Palestinian population centers, (2)
shorten the line between settlement areas and the Green Line,
and (3) develop a sense of community among the various settlement blocs, all the while keeping Palestinian traffic away from
the settlements. The roads help define what Israel would claim
during any final status talks. That Palestinian traffic, always limited by the few on- and off-ramps in Palestinian communities, was
substantially eliminated during the Second Intifada has added the
insult of inconvenience to the injury caused by the fact that many
of the roads were built in substantial part on privately owned
Palestinian lands. Although Israeli law prohibits the construction
of settlements on those lands, military seizures for security-related reasons are harder to challenge.

Jerusalem, where the Second Intifada was born, remains a

21. Dror Etkes, Danny Seidemann, and Ir Amim, "What is E-1," *Settlements in Focus*, Peace Now/Americans for Peace Now, May 2005, p. 1.

place vulnerable to bad decisions and allergic responses. Since the Gaza withdrawals, the local Palestinian focus has returned to two Jerusalem-related issues. The first, now on hold, involves a plan by the municipality to demolish eighty-eight Palestinian homes on the southern edge of the Old City called Silwan. The area, believed to have once been occupied by King David, has been zoned for parkland purposes and is now central to city plans for an archeological park around the Old City. Standing alone, the controversy would sear few nerves and quickly pass away, but few things stand alone in the history of Israeli-Palestinian relations, particularly when it comes to Jerusalem.

Nor are events there divorced from personalities. Ariel Sharon, for example, has been at the center of a number of incendiary events involving Jerusalem. Sharon was minister of agriculture in 1982 when he established a special committee whose purpose was to help militant settler groups use government land to establish a foothold at a site near Herod's Gate. As minister of housing in 1991, he tried unsuccessfully to fast-track a similar effort. That same year, a board of inquiry headed by Haim Klugman, director general of the Ministry of Justice, placed Sharon at the center of a series of policies described in a Peace Now report as "tainted by systemic and blatant illegality." Government assets had been funneled illegally to settler groups, which also used falsified documents to seize Palestinian properties. Later, it was as minister of infrastructure in 1998 that Sharon supported settler groups trying to undertake construction at Herod's Gate, a move then being blocked by the Israeli courts. As prime minister, Sharon's failure to meaningfully attack the problem of illegal settlements on the West Bank grated on both Palestinian and American nerves. He was publicly committed to their demolition and was obligated by the first stage of the Road Map document to do so, just as the Palestinian leadership is to dismantle the apparatus of terrorism in its own society. Overall, Palestinians suspected he was selective in his observance of the law and one-sided in demanding their adherence to cease-fires and confidence-building security measures while ignoring those he saw as inconvenient.

"Sharon underwent a change in the way he looked at settlements," claims an Israeli who frequently participated in meetings with him. "Until he decided to disengage, he didn't care about illegal settlements. Once he changed policy, the illegal settlements became important."[22]

One of the important early decisions of the Olmert government will be to define and execute Israeli policy as regards illegal settlement activity. In 2003, perhaps to lay the political groundwork for addressing the issue, Sharon asked a lawyer named Talya Sason to investigate the status of the illegal settlements or, as they are frequently called, "outposts." Her comprehensive report was issued in March 2005.[23] In it, she documented the practice of establishing the illegal settlements, checked their then-current status, and identified a figure of 105 such outposts, with at least twenty-four having been built after Sharon became prime minister. Peace Now, which has kept track of the growth of illegal settlements for years, has placed their number at over one hundred with just over fifty planted during Sharon's period in office. As such sources document, the practice first gained impetus after 1993 when Yitzhak Rabin froze new settlement construction on the West Bank and Gaza. Although most illegal outposts started with delivery of a single caravan to a desired location, several now have multiple caravans; many have the permanent structures—administrative centers, classrooms, even homes—which have replaced the early caravans.[24]

22. Interview with senior Israeli participant, January 2006. By mutual agreement, the conversation was on background.
23. Talya Sason, "Summary of the Opinion Concerning Unauthorized Outposts," Prime Minister's Office, Communications Department, Israel, March 10, 2005.
24. Ibid.

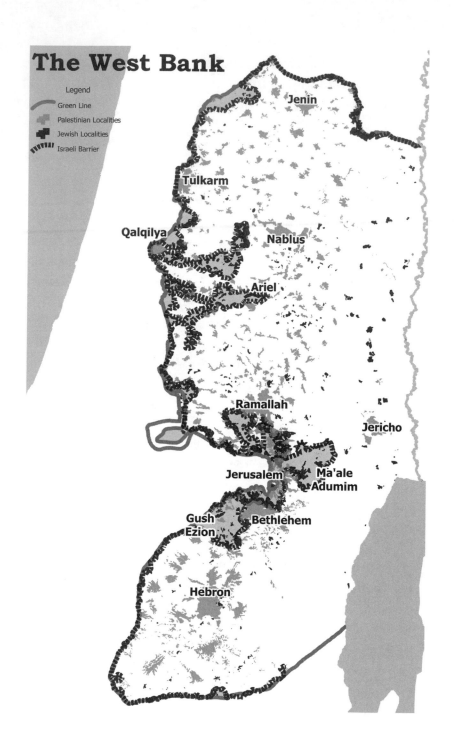

The West Bank

Legend

⌒ Green Line

▨ Palestinian Localities

◼ Jewish Localities

⸾⸾⸾⸾ Israeli Barrier

Jenin

Tulkarm

Qalqilya

Nablus

Ariel

Ramallah

Jericho

Jerusalem

Ma'ale Adumim

Gush Ezion

Bethlehem

Hebron

Sason found a pattern of covert and, in many cases, illegal dealings with the government as typical of the settlement issue over the years. A paralyzed policy emerged as the law ran in one direction and the Zionist ethic in another. That is, those committed to the idea of settlements were far more dedicated to building them than were authorities charged with oversight in stopping them. She found no single agency keeping tabs on the illegal activity while some agencies were in active collusion with the law breakers.

Ms. Sason found the Ministry of Construction and Housing a particular culprit. Not only did it knowingly distribute funds to illegal outposts but it cooked the books by entering the funds in an account whose purpose was expansion and improvement of existing lawful settlements. Further, the Settlement Division of the World Zionist Organization was systematically establishing illegal outposts. Shockingly, she also found some fifteen settlements situated on private Palestinian land, a practice held illegal since an Israeli Supreme Court decision in the late 1970s. In some cases the illegal activities amounted to felonies, but no court had the criminal jurisdiction to try the case. And when authorities would finally exercise the gumption to dismantle an illegal outpost, often the settlers would return in a flash, picking up where they had left off before being interrupted.

According to Ms. Sason, "The big picture is a bold violation of laws by certain State authorities, public authorities, regional councils in Judea, Samaria and Gaza and settlers, while falsely presenting an organized legal system."[25]

Still, there seems little doubt that the illegal outposts will be gone once the dust settles. They have no strategic value. All are in areas from which the Israelis will certainly withdraw. The demands of the United States, the commitments of Israel, and the

25. Ibid.

insistence of the broader international community are so clear
and the political costs of the outposts relative to their strategic
worth so great that one has trouble envisioning a contrary outcome. Olmert's approach to the issue was exhibited February 1,
2006, when, pursuant to court approval, he ordered security
forces to dismantle the illegal settlement of Amona located near
Ramallah. A gathering of settler protesters estimated at two thousand hurled rocks and paint at the security forces, set roofs afire
and employed wooden stakes to push back the troops, but they
were outmanned and out-equipped. Residents—their numbers
swelled many times over by youthful out-of-area protesters—were
pulled kicking and screaming from the houses. Local officials and
medical personnel estimated the number of injuries at about
eighty. In office less than a month, Olmert had shown he could
act decisively against militant West Bank settlers, particularly
where the issue is illegal outposts. But, particularly in the midst
of an election campaign, he did not seek confrontation for its own
sake. Perhaps the outposts give him a few cards to play in order
to pre-empt more serious demands. Or perhaps he is delighted to
have Israel's Road Map noncompliance juxtaposed with that of
the Palestinians, entangled as they are with the far more difficult
terrorism issue.

Today's numbers on the West Bank underline the fact that,
the Gaza disengagement notwithstanding, demographics remain
an issue of central Israeli concern. Not counting East Jerusalem,
an estimated two-hundred-and-thirty-five thousand settlers reside
in a total of 121 West Bank settlements, compared to about 2.5
million Palestinians also living on the West Bank. The vast majority of settlers—160,000 to 175,000 residing in fifty-one settlements—live inside the projected area of the security fence. This
leaves seventy-three settlements and about seventy thousand settlers outside the protective shield of the security barrier. (Counting only settlements approved by the government, the highly re-

spected Center for Mid-east Peace and Economic Cooperation places the number of settlers residing east of the proposed security barrier at 58,000.) If unilateral separation means nothing else, it means that, one way or another, their communities are at risk. Either through further unilateral steps or final status negotiations, Israel will have to find a way to protect its own territory inside the Green Line, retain its Jerusalem area settlement blocs, provide a formula for dividing the land that will satisfy a working majority of its own citizens, and give Palestinian leaders something they can present to their constituencies—including their own diaspora and other states in the region—without providing a new *casus belli*.

Yet the key geographic areas of contention all have special histories or relate to important current issues. Ariel may be in the heart of the West Bank, but it is a well-run, modern, secular Israeli town that embodies the values of historic Zionism. Hebron and Kiryat Arba are open sores on the corpus of Palestinian society. But Hebron, the City of Patriarchs, is nearly as precious to Jews as Jerusalem, and they have paid a very high price to return to a city their ancestors inhabited through more than two millennia. Efrat, a pleasant community that gets along well with Palestinian neighbors is also another obstacle blocking the Palestinian dream of a capital in East Jerusalem. In this sense, the hard times of Intifada 2 have made it necessary for both sides to abandon policies grounded in the sawdust of illusion. The dragon of Greater Israel was slain by one of its principal architects even as the tactic of suicidal terrorism turned out to be very expensive for those who borrowed it from more extreme allies and made it their weapon of choice.

7. Politics and Diplomacy

AS ISRAELI FORCES were clearing recalcitrant settlers from their Gaza homes on August 16, 2005, Khalil Shikaki, director of the Palestinian Center for Policy and Survey Research (PSR) in Ramallah, published a column in the *Jerusalem Post* headlined, "How Sharon and Abbas Can Both Win."[1] Shikaki, a pollster and political analyst respected in Israel and the west, questioned the wisdom of Israeli unilateralism in Gaza and on the West Bank as opposed to Lebanon, where no one on the other side wanted to talk. Here, he argued, Hamas may be as close-minded as Hezbollah, preferring to paint Israel's withdrawal as a victory for Palestinian resistance, but Abu Mazen, supported by Palestinian public opinion, wanted to reduce tensions and negotiate. Make him look good by easing restrictions on Palestinian trade and movement, and he will help Sharon and Israel by defeating Hamas and talking about the terms for settling the conflict. In other words, let the PA rather than Hamas control the Palestinian narrative of withdrawal.

Shakaki updated his survey data two months later for a conference at Brandeis University hosted by Shai Feldman, director of the Crown Center for Middle East Studies and former director of the Jaffee Center for Strategic Studies in Tel Aviv. By that October conference, 84 percent of Palestinians were convinced that violence had played a role in the Israeli withdrawal. Irre-

1. Khalil Shikaki, "How Sharon and Abbas Can Both Win," *Jerusalem Post*, August 16, 2005.

spective of this faith in the efficacy of violence, however, the percentage of Palestinians willing to compromise on final status issues had grown from 25 percent in 1996 to 35–40 percent after Camp David to 55–60 percent after the Gaza pullout. Meanwhile, the needle of popular support for Hamas seemed stuck in the mid-high 20s, though it was later shown rising. Shikaki interpreted the Palestinian message to Hamas pointedly: "Thank you very much. Now go home."[2]

Looking back after the January 2006 elections, Shikaki's words have a quaint "Dewey beats Truman" ring. His message, however, was not fundamentally different from the sort of practical, humanistic "day after" advice the Sharon government was receiving from many sources including the PA, left-of-center Israelis, the Europeans, and Condoleezza Rice. Abu Mazen and his PA were the last best hope for solving the problem. Yet Abu Mazen lacked a strong political base. His one hope, then, was to demonstrate effectiveness through making people's lives better. That meant convincing the Israelis to move quickly on an assortment of issues that made a difference.

In reality, Israel's cooperation proved grudging, piecemeal, and incomplete, reflecting the judgment of its political leadership that Abbas was a losing horse. Sharon's political position inside Israel grew strong enough for him to move with apparent success toward a major overhaul of the country's political structure.[3] Abu Mazen, on the other hand, suffered one personal setback after another, to the point where younger leaders of his own Fatah Party offered their own slate of legislative candidates, discarding Abbas' prime minister, Ahmed Qurei.[4] Atop their new slate was

2. Speech presented by Khalil Shikaki on October 20, 2005, at Brandeis University, Crown Center for Middle East Studies, "Israel and the Palestinians: The Road Ahead."

3. See, for example, Steven Erlanger and Greg Myre, "Sharon's New Party Shuffles the Political Deck, Setting Off a Scramble for Israeli Elections," New York Times, November 22, 2005.

4. See, for example, Conal Urquhart, "Fatah Faces Split as Militant Leader

Marwan Barghouti, presently serving five consecutive life sentences in an Israeli jail for planning terrorist operations executed by his Tanzim militia during the Second Intifada that killed a total of five people. But even Barghouti was not enough to stop what turned out to be a massive and stunning Hamas victory. Why events unfolded as they did helps clarify the situation in both the Israeli and Palestinian camps and define what one can look for in the period ahead.

First, it is worth repeating that unilateral separation came about not because a cooperative Palestinian faction was waiting in the wings but, to the contrary, because Israelis in large numbers had concluded there was no Palestinian partner with whom to negotiate. When Sharon first announced his plan for unilateral territorial moves, Yasser Arafat was running Fatah, the PLO, and the PA. He had been thoroughly discredited in the eyes of most Israelis as a recidivist terrorist whose pretensions to the contrary during the Oslo years had proven a pack of lies. Abu Mazen had been plucked from early if comfortable retirement, whisked off, and made prime minister. He quit after a few months, principally because Arafat wanted no division of power. True, after Arafat's death Abu Mazen had been elected in a fair vote. Yet although the position had been conferred on him, real power had not. Thus, while several matters—ranging from what to do with the settlers' homes to how Palestinians could travel between Gaza and the West Bank—demanded consultation with the Israelis and some give and take, they were not negotiations in any sense of the word; they involved no quid pro quo. Israel's responsibility for unilaterally ensuring its own interests was magnified, though some coordination with the PA at places such as the Rafah crossing remined essential.

Second, as the principal critique of the unilateral pullback

Quits to Set Up Rival Movement: Palestinian Young Guard Out to Modernise Party: President Tries to Appease Rebels without Success," *The Guardian*, December 16, 2005.

plan was that it would reward—and hence encourage—terrorism, Sharon tried to ensure that the pullback itself generated no new security problems. Take the issue of the Rafah crossing along the Philadelphi Corridor separating Egypt from Gaza. Even under Israeli control, the crossing became a flashpoint for the smuggling of weapons into Gaza through tunnels dug from the Egyptian side. Terrorists sought by the Israelis also on occasion found their way through the tunnels. With the Israelis now pulling back, who would police the border? If not the Israelis, could they at least monitor the checkpoint in real time? Using what equipment? Who would make the decision as to whether a particular individual was free to cross? In the end, with the prodding of U.S. secretary of state Condoleezza Rice and the motivation provided by a couple of all-night bargaining sessions, the parties came close enough to agreement to permit Rafah to reopen on November 25. The result: the border is presently under PA control and its officers have the final say over who can cross; the Israelis monitor the proceedings via live surveillance cameras; Egypt and teams of European observers patrol Egypt's side of the border. Here, as we shall see shortly, from the vantage of security, the deal worked poorly. The price of guns in the area—a good indicator of smuggling trade success—fell to the lowest point in years. And in a truly ugly incident, two Egyptian troops were shot and killed as a Palestinian mob, angered by the slow clearance pace, surged across the border into Egypt while another commandeered a front-end loader and began smashing down a restraining wall. Israelis, now safely out of Gaza, barely blinked. They had suspected all along that Abu Mazen was not a man who people feared to cross.

The Karni crossing is a third illustration of the clash between Israeli security and Palestinian mobility. Karni had long been the exit point for fruits and vegetables produced by Palestinian farmers. With the coming of the Second Intifada, Karni became a target of Palestinian terrorist attacks. The Israelis, therefore, became even more security conscious both at the Karni crossing and at the points of final destination, a concern that was underlined when militants attempted unsuccessfully to blow up the crossing. Palestinians soon faced economic loss if not disaster. They complained of multiple cargo transfers and inspection delays resulting in spoiled merchandise. And that was just to get to the far side of the checkpoint! Once on the West Bank, the trucks were subjected to the same delays as resident Palestinian vehicles. The Israelis recommended that the produce be transported in shipping containers, making goods far easier to monitor. But they were in short supply. So trucks continued to ply the roads, accompanied by multiple inspections, the cargo transfers, and delays. More often than not, Palestinian farmers would have been better off destroying whatever portion of the produce could not be sold or consumed locally, yet another example of the terrorism surtax that survived even after Intifada 2 withered away.

A final area of Rice-induced accommodation involved Israel's agreement to permit bus convoys carrying Palestinians to travel between Gaza and Tarqumiya on the West Bank beginning December 15, 2005. At Israeli insistence, no one between sixteen and thirty-five may be a passenger, the travelers must be Gaza residents, and all must return to Gaza within ten days. Yet despite such security measures, by year's end the service had still to begin. According to a military spokesman, given the "situation in Gaza when rockets are still flying from Gaza to Israel, and all these security problems it is the decision of the minister of defense that until the situation is quiet, we won't go ahead with the convoys."[5] One can only imagine the nature of Israeli cooperation on these sensitive border issues with Hamas now in power.

Sharon might have had more incentive to help Abbas had the Palestinian chairman shown any inclination to tackle Hamas, PIJ,

---

5. Steven Erlanger, "No Buses Roll from Gaza to West Bank, Despite Deal," *New York Times*, December 31, 2005.

or even Fatah's own rebellious militias. But the most he could extract from them was a "period of calm," and even that was punctuated by suicide bombs, targeted raids, and Qassan rockets fired from abandoned settlements in Gaza toward Sderot, Ashkelon, and other sites inside the Green Line. Subsequently, Israel declared in late December the northern strip of Gaza a "no go" zone—similar to the "free fire" zones of the Vietnam era—subject to perpetual reconnaissance and attack in an effort to push the Palestinian rockets out of range. By then, the list of "day after" lifestyle improvements that could help Abbas and Fatah overcome the Hamas challenge was far from Israeli minds.

The Israeli leader was also engaged in a fierce struggle within his own party. Likud was deeply conflicted. This was the successor to Herut, the party of Vladimir Jabotinsky, a secular advocate of Greater Israel. Jabotinsky believed conquest of the nation from its resident Arab population would free the Jewish spirit and toughen the Jewish character, just as defeating the Native American tribes who stood in the path of America's westward expansion had provided that nation of immigrants with one of its unifying myths. It was also the party of Menachem Begin, the man who had made settling Judea and Samaria a national policy. Of course, Jabotinsky died in 1940, an also-ran in the struggle for primacy against David Ben Gurion, and Begin had been overcome with depression as Israel's push into Lebanon turned increasingly sour.

More to the contemporary debate, as prime minister, Bibi Netanyahu had pulled back from most of the Hebron area and signed the Wye Accord restoring Palestinian self-rule to 97 percent of its population. Netanyahu also endorsed, albeit with reservations, the Sharon pullback. His last-minute objections to the plan, which led to his resignation from Sharon's cabinet just before its final vote on the pullout, made him appear more Machiavelli than Jabotinsky or Begin. But if the split between Sharon and the hard-line Likudniks had become hard to define in purely philosophical terms, the combination of history and political emotion made it painful nonetheless.

Sharon had little time to fret about the hard times Palestinians faced in Gaza. He needed reasonable quiet to contemplate his political moves. Should he stay with the Likud through the nominating convention in December or bolt early? With only 52 percent of the vote, he had narrowly defeated an effort by Likud opponents to move up the party primary. The tightness of that contest reflected the deep fractures within his party. But the win also conveyed the sense of many party members that Likud could only win with Sharon atop the ticket. Now he was running neck and neck with Netanyahu among Likud voters even as he outdistanced Bibi in polls positioning him as an independent party candidate. Was it time to complete the long political march begun with the 2003 speech at Herzyliya? Unless he moved swiftly, he might have to move as a loser in the Likud primary.

Sharon also wanted to parlay his withdrawal from Gaza into concrete diplomatic gains. Israel has always defined these as garnering increased support from the United States while reducing its isolation elsewhere. In these respects, Sharon was something of a diplomatic bus driver, rolling his vehicle some distance down the road, collecting fares, rolling to the next stop, collecting additional fares, and so forth. By the time the final cabinet vote loomed, he had already collected his fare from the United States, getting Washington to renounce the Palestinian refugee right of return to Israel and to reject any obligation for Israel to return to the precise 1967 borders. Then in July 2005, the broader diplomatic offensive began with a visit to France and some high-visibility, low-content meetings with President Jacques Chirac. Weeks earlier the trip seemed in jeopardy when Sharon invited French Jews to emigrate in order to skirt rampant anti-Semitism in France, but the insult was paved over when Sharon withdrew the reference and Chirac denounced both anti-Semitism and terror-ism.

More significant was the late August meeting in Ankara be-tween Israeli foreign minister Sylvan Shalom and his Pakistani counterpart, Khurghid Kasuri, a meeting that the latter explicitly linked to the Gaza pullout. The meeting was organized by Turkish prime minister Recep Tayyep Erdogen with Pakistan also seeking and obtaining endorsements of the initiative from Abu Mazen and King Abdullah of Saudi Arabia. Pakistan made it clear that it had no plans to establish formal diplomatic relations with Israel until a Palestinian state is established with its capital in Jerusalem. Regardless, Mr. Shalom still said the get-together had "tremen-dous significance, not just in our relationship with Pakistan, but the entire Muslim world."[6]

Sharon addressed the UN General Assembly on September 15.[7] The speech was filled with personal testimony of Sharon's relationship with the land and his deep love of "sowing and har-vesting, the pastures, the flock and the cattle." Reaching an emo-tional eloquence and depth rarely found in his domestic talks—including those dealing with the Gaza withdrawal—he captured the difficulty of giving up even part the land: "Every inch of land, every hill and valley, every stream and rock, is saturated with Jewish history, replete with memories." Still, he fully acknowl-edged, Palestinians also live there and "Palestinians will always be our neighbors. We respect them and have no aspirations to rule over them. They are also entitled to freedom and to a na-tional, sovereign existence in a state of their own." That was the first time an Israeli prime minister embraced Palestinian state-hood before an international body. There was no letting the

6. Silvan Shalom, "Pakistan-Israel in Landmark Talks," BBC News, Thursday, September 1, 2005, 14:49 GMT, 15:49 UK.

7. Ariel Sharon, prime minister (Israel), Speech to United Nations, "Now the Palestinians Must Prove Their Desire for Peace," September 15, 2005.

Palestinians off the hook on their single most important commitment, however; "The most important test the Palestinian leadership will face is in fulfilling their commitment to put an end to terrorism and its infrastructures, eliminate the anarchic regime of armed gangs and cease the incitement and indoctrination of hatred towards Israel and the Jews."[8]

On October 11, 2005, the *New York Times* reported on the vastly improved atmosphere at the UN with respect to Israel. For example, the article observed that "Israel recently proposed a United Nations resolution, it submitted its candidacy for a two-year seat on the Security Council, and its prime minister has been warmly received speaking to the General Assembly."[9] The report credited Secretary General Kofi Annan for reducing Israel's marginalization, through such measures as a seminar on anti-Semitism, a resolution condemning the same, a special ceremony commemorating the liberation of the Nazi death camps, and Secretary Annan's own decision to address a ceremony at the opening of a new wing at the Yad Vashem memorial in Jerusalem. These developments may not be directly linked to the Gaza pullout, but it would be hard to imagine any of them occurring before Sharon's Herzyliya speech and the resulting steps toward withdrawal.

Previously on September 30, the *New York Times* correspondent in Kuwait filed a report indicating that Kuwaitis were actively debating their long-standing efforts to isolate Israel and considering revisions in the policy.[10] The editor in chief of the English-language paper *The Arab Times* was quoted in the article as saying, "We Arabs have also reached a unanimous agreement to make peace with Israel as our strategic choice, before con-

8. Ibid.

9. Warren Hoge, "U.N. Is Gradually Becoming More Hospitable to Israel," *New York Times*, October 11, 2005.

10. Hassan M. Fattah, "Kuwaitis Quietly Breach a Taboo: Easing Hostility Toward Israel," *New York Times*, October 5, 2005.

ducting negotiations with that country."[11] Referring specifically
to the Gaza withdrawal, a Saudi journalist residing in Kuwait
wrote, "Normalizing ties with Israel is an important event, and
its positive effect will permeate every aspect of the Arab political,
economic, cultural and social life."[12]

Egyptian president Hosni Mubarak was not an early advocate
of Israel's unilateral disengagement plan. To the contrary, as he
argued in an April 2004 visit with President Bush at the latter's
Texas ranch, by letting Israel do what it was comfortable doing
without any Palestinian input, the move virtually preempted the
possibility of real progress with the Road Map or in any other
forum.[13] The fix was already in, however. While Mubarak dallied
in Texas, the president returned to Washington for a meeting with
Sharon at which he endorsed the plan; he further rewarded
Sharon by bestowing a general blessing on Israeli West Bank settlement blocs.

Recognizing the futility of his initial plea, Mubarak thereupon
launched an initiative designed to address his strategic concerns
regarding the move, specifically his belief that it would turn Gaza
into a bitter, impoverished and isolated "Hamastan" whose radicals would infiltrate Egypt, causing untold mischief. This would
constitute an unstable situation that could ultimately threaten his
regime. The October 2004 terrorist attacks in Taba and Nuweiba
served to underline for Mubarak the generally small number and
low quality of his forces in the area. He responded by returning
Ambassador Mohamad Bassiouni to Tel Aviv with an offer to help
train, arm, and equip any PA security forces needed to keep other
militias in check. Mr. Bassiouni, who had been home for "consultations" since the Second Intifada broke out in 2000, also

11. Ibid.

12. Ibid.

13. Ayellet Yehiav, "The Egyptians at Philadelphi: Regional Interests, Local
Challenges," *Strategic Assessment* 8, no. 3 (November 2005).

helped organize the official December 2004 signing of a Qualified Industrial Zones agreement whereby certain goods produced by Egypt using components made in Israel are permitted into the United States duty free. Mr. Mubarak further offered support for the PA by sending an ambassador to Ramallah, the West Bank administrative capital.[14]

In March 2005, Mubarak hosted the Cairo Conference involving Fatah, Hamas, and eleven splinter factions focused on determining what to do in the face of Israel's planned Gaza withdrawal. The gathering decided to institute a period of calm.[15] Despite some firing on Israeli targets by Hamas early in the summer of 2005, the part of the deal relating to Israel worked rather well. It would be Palestinian versus Palestinian violence that would get out of hand.

Mubarak subsequently concluded this round of participation by agreeing to install a force of 750 troops to help police the entire Philadelphi Corridor, replacing the departing Israelis.[16] From one who had gone to Washington hoping to block the unilateral disengagement, Mubarak had led Egypt into a position of substantial utility, a clear triumph for Sharon's diplomacy.

There was, however, a downside to the Cairo Conference. To achieve the consent of Hamas to the *tahdiya* (period of calm), Abu Mazen had agreed to legislative council elections with favorable ground rules, allowed Hamas to field candidates without disbanding its militia, renouncing terrorism, or agreeing to abide by the Oslo Accords. He also issued a powerful statement committing his government never to compromise on the absolute

---

14. Ibid.

15. See, for example, Molly Moore, "Militants Extend Pledge Not to Attack Israel," *Washington Post*, March 18, 2005.

16. See, for example, Margot Dudkevitch and Orly Halpern, "Egypt Deploys at Philadelphi," *Jerusalem Post*, September 11, 2005; and Thanassis Cambanis and Anne Barnard, "After Gaza Pullout, Egypt Border Is New Division," *Boston Globe*, September 18, 2005.

right of Palestinian refugees to return to Israel. Thus Mubarak's bias toward a negotiated end to the Israeli-Palestinian dispute started a chain of events, leading to formal commitment by Abu Mazen, making that result impossible to reach. Plus, in yielding on the question of private militias, Abu Mazen had so diminished Israel's stake in the outcome of Palestinian elections as to negate the likelihood of serious cooperation on the quality-of-life issues.

On September 21, 2005, Jordan's king Abdullah II hosted a gathering of approximately seventy rabbis whom he flew to Washington, urging Jews and Muslims to "take bold steps toward mutual forgiveness and reconciliation."[17] The gathering was apparently the king's follow-up to a declaration issued during the celebration of Ramadan denouncing terrorism practiced under the banner of Islam. At an international conference convened by Abdullah in July, 180 Muslim religious leaders from both the Sunni and Shiite branches denounced the issuance of fatwas by those acting outside traditional practice. As the king explained: "Muslims from every branch of Islam can now assert without doubt or hesitation that a fatwah calling for the killing of innocent civilians—no matter what nationality or religion, Muslim or Jew, Arab or Israeli—is a violation of the most fundamental principles of Islam."[18] Weeks later, when suicide bomb attacks on three Amman hotels killed fifty-seven civilians, thousands of Jordanians took to the streets to demonstrate their disgust at the murders.

Overall, Israel's withdrawal from Gaza was clearly the proximate cause of the Mubarak initiative and most likely a substantial factor in Kuwait's reassessment and King Abdullah's anti-terrorism campaign. Both Egypt and Jordan have made strategic decisions—largely based on their need for good relations with Washington—to develop normal relations with Israel and both can

17. Charles A Radin, "Jordan's King Extends Hand to Jews," *Boston Globe*, September 22, 2005.
    18. Ibid.

benefit from cooperative dealings with the Israelis in countering regional terrorist threats. Kuwait may be at an earlier stage in the same diplomatic evolution. Israeli actions that are viewed in the region as positive make it easier for Egypt, Jordan, and Kuwait to do what their interests suggest. Periods of heightened tension, on the other hand, turn these relationships into ones characterized by the term "cold peace."

In party elections conducted during the second week of November, Israel's Labor Party stunned the country, Ariel Sharon, and itself by ousting Sharon's coalition partner Shimon Peres as its leader and electing in his stead Amir Peretz. Here was the left-wing director of the Histadrut union, an avowed "peacenik" who conceives of the occupation as immoral. Above all, he was avowedly committed to taking Labor out of Peres' coalition alliance with Likud and made this a central tenet of his campaign.

Peretz is a man easily underestimated but not easily over-simplified. With his open-necked blue sport-shirts and thick Stalinist moustache, he looks like a transplanted '30s-style radical. He is Moroccan by birth, one of the ethnic groups that formed the core of Menachem Begin's Sephardi constituency. As refugees from the Arab world they were poor, but Labor's intellectual socialism and European orientation never reached them. Peretz wants to change that. "This is the moment we bury the ethnic demon in Israel," he told his supporters. To another interviewer, Peretz asserted, "I would like to be the Menachem Begin of the Labor Party, to return it to the social values and support of the people. If I receive from the people the same 'train ticket' that they once gave to Begin, I intend to travel with it towards peace."[19] He speaks of occupation in words rarely heard since the start of Intifada 2, describing it as "an immoral act, first of all.

19. Ami Isseroff, "Biography of Amir Peretz," Zionism and Israel—Biographies, *The Encyclopedia and Dictionary of Zionism and Israel.*

The occupation in my view is not a territorial question, but one of morality. I want to end the occupation not because of international or Palestinian pressure, but because I see it as an Israeli interest."[20]

Coalition politics plays funny games with the most ideological of people. When the March election made Kadima and Labor the two largest Knesset blocs, Olmert asked Peretz to serve in his cabinet, as defense minister no less. Peretz suddenly appeared content to keep some West Bank settlements on the basis of unilateral action instead of his cherished negotiations.

The essence of Sharon's planning for the months ahead thus came quickly into focus. First, leave the Likud. Second, cast the broadest possible net so that the new party—which he soon named "Kadima" (Forward)—wins enough Knesset seats not only to beat Likud, but to also make himself and not Peretz the logical choice to form a new government. Third, sit tight on the West Bank while awaiting the summons to begin Road Map talks. Fourth, use the PA's inability to dismantle the infrastructure of terrorist organizations and the rising political power of Hamas to resist pressure that may develop for a rapid and unsatisfactory deal. Fifth, use the security wall and other construction to create facts on the ground with respect to the settlements he wanted to keep and Jerusalem, which he did not wish to share. Such should have helped him wear down the Palestinian leadership to the point where they would be willing to make pivotal concessions on such issues as the West Bank settlement blocs and the right of Palestinian refugees to return to Israel. In the end, Sharon would have defined the borders of the Jewish state of Israel.

Sharon's decision to leave the Likud produced stunning initial numbers. A poll published in *Yediot Achronnot*—the nation's larg-

---

20. BBC News, "Profile: Amir Peretz," 13 November 2005, 12:59 GMT.

est daily—showed Kadima winning thirty-three Knesset seats, Labor garnering twenty-six, and the Likud falling off a cliff from its current forty seats to twelve. Kadima climbed even higher in the weeks that followed before appearing to settle in the mid–high thirties. Astonishingly, after Sharon's massive stroke, Kadima climbed to over forty Knesset mandates in the polls, though one suspected that once Netanyahu began playing the theme that unilateral disengagement had turned Hamas into a dangerous power, the spread would narrow. Shimon Peres announced he was leaving Labor to support Sharon after a political association of well over half a century. He was soon running high on the Kadima ticket, a candidate for deputy prime minister. Further, Sharon appeared to be draining Likud of its top leadership. Defense Minister Shaul Mofaz, the Iranian-born hard-liner, first declared his candidacy for the top spot in the Likud. But when he continued to trail Netanyahu badly, Mofaz—obviously banking on a senior cabinet post in the next government—joined Sharon. To the consternation of his former mates, so too did Tzachi Hanegbi, one of only five cabinet ministers to have voted in August against authorizing the pullout to begin. At the time of his defection, Hanegbi was serving as head of the Likud Central Committee and acting party chairman. He offered a disarmingly candid explanation for his move: "What Sharon will do in the next four years won't be done by any national leader in the next 30 years."[21]

On December 18, 2005, Sharon suffered a mild stroke while driving to his farm in the Negev. Doctors at the Hadassah-Ein Kerem Hospital in Jerusalem described the stroke as nondebilitating, but days later announced that a small hole had been found in the prime minister's heart—the likely cause of the blood clot

---

21. Robert Rosenberg, "Every Man for Himself," *Today's Situation from Ariga*, December 7, 2005.

responsible for the stroke—and that a procedure had been scheduled for January 5 to repair it. Mr. Sharon had been put on blood-
thinner medication to prevent further clotting. Upon learning of
the initial stroke, jubilant Palestinian militia members in Gaza
celebrated by firing their weapons into the air; a seemingly
breathless commentator on the *Haaretz* website predicted that,
were Sharon to be removed by illness from the scene, "the entire
political system would be thrown into an insane whirlwind re-
shuffling all the cards."[22] Then, on January 4, 2006, the day before his scheduled minor procedure, Sharon suffered a massive
debilitating stroke and hemorrhage, removing him from the political scene. Olmert became acting prime minister and would
soon be chosen to replace Sharon atop the Kadima ticket. Supporters of unilateral disengagement feared the worst.

There are, however, a number of reasons to suggest that
much of the early "cult of the personality" analysis was off base.
True Sharon had enormous physical magnetism—the hospital
listed him as 5 feet, 7 inches tall and 318 pounds. True he had
great political energy. True he had freed Israel form the jaws of
Intifada 2 while engaging international support by withdrawing
from the Gaza Strip. And true he had brought into being an apparently viable political party formed in his own image.

Even before he left Likud, however, many close observers of
the political scene were crediting Sharon less with having in-
vented a new political constituency than with having located and
awoken the dormant political center. Perhaps the most astute of
these observers is Yehuda Ben-Meir, a veteran of the National
Religious Party, former Knesset member, and commentator on the
fusion of religion and politics in Israeli society.

22. Greg Myre, "A Mild Stroke Sends Sharon to the Hospital," *New York
Times*, December 19, 2005.

Addressing the Brandeis conference in October 2005, Ben-Meir suggested that, during his five years in office, Sharon had found the political majority even as they had found him. With his disengagement initiative, he had "broken the genetic code" of the new Israeli majority just as Franklin Roosevelt, in an earlier day, had broken through isolationism with lend-lease and the destroyer deal to find the genetic code of the new internationalism.

Ben-Meir offered six conclusions that Sharon and the New Center had reached as part of their union, each pointing toward a policy initiative:

1. They were disillusioned with the Palestinians as negotiating partners. This owed itself to the rise of terrorist organizations alongside the PA's fragmentation, corruption, and inability to provide law and order, all embodied in the ineffectual presidency of Abu Mazen. Per this assessment, Israel cannot wait for the Palestinians to begin fixing things before addressing pressing occupation-related issues.

2. There existed the conviction that demography outweighs geography. The Israeli settlement policy must reflect the fact that the question is not what God defined as the Land of Israel, but who lives there now. With Palestinians growing faster than Jewish Israelis, the character of the state is at risk and needs to be secured.

3. Separation remains the essence of Israeli policy. As Rabin once declared, "We are here; they are there." The security fence is supported among Israelis polled, by 82.4 percent, and will continue.

4. After Gaza, future unilateral withdrawals are fraught with danger. The Palestinians see them as rewards for terrorism. Their response will be to practice more terrorism, and so fu-

ture disengagements must be considered as a measure affecting security both as a fact on the ground and as it relates to the perception of the other side.

5. When Israel does take unilateral steps, it is entitled to something in return from third parties. Israel received at least two important declarations from President Bush. Additional support should accompany additional steps as part of a quid pro quo.

6. Defense and security preclude a complete return to the 1967 borders. The big settlement blocs must be kept as vital to Israeli security interests. Paradoxically, however, long-run and pervasive security can only be achieved by a negotiated peace.[23]

One can quibble with particular items on Ben-Meir's list. The belief, for example, that future unilateral disengagement is fraught with danger may come as a surprise to Mr. Olmert, who endorsed the concept in his preelection "convergences" address, in which he said he would seek to determine Israel's final borders unilaterally during his four-year term. And getting nice things from the United States hardly seems like cracking a political genome code. But Ben-Meir's overall thesis—that Sharon and an apparent Israeli plurality of the center seemed to find each other on a range of security issues during his five years in office and that this agreement produced extremely strong political ties—is fundamentally on point. The question of whether these ties are being institutionalized through the new mechanism of Kadima to the point where they will survive both the sudden removal of Sharon from the scene and the earthquake of the January 2006

23. Speech presented by Yehuda Ben-Meir on October 20, 2005, at Brandeis University, Crown Center for Middle East Studies, "Israel and the Palestinians: The Road Ahead."

Hamas electoral victory, may or may not have been answered by the campaign itself. If the American experience is any example, one may argue that the collective security approach developed by Franklin Roosevelt to run the Second World War had been institutionalized by war's end, leading to a seamless hand-off to Harry Truman. Had Sharon remained personally on the political scene, no answer to the question need immediately have been sought. Now that he is gone, it has suddenly become the dominant question in Israeli politics. In the new situation, Olmert could become an Israeli Harry Truman. On the other hand, he could instead become an Israeli Andrew Johnson, whose inability to institutionalize Abraham Lincoln's vision of a forgiving but just reconstruction helped doom the nation to a century of racial and sectional grief.

On December 15, 2005, Hamas dealt a punishing blow to Fatah and the PA with a strong showing in municipal elections conducted on the West Bank, signaling what was to come in the legislative council elections of January 2006. The former organization—branded as a terrorist group by Israel, the United States, and the European Union—won thirteen of the fifteen seats up for grabs in Nablus, squeaked by in Jenin, and easily won in El Bireh, a suburb of Ramallah, while Fatah prevailed in Ramallah proper. Overall, Fatah captured 35 percent of the seats at stake while Hamas secured 26 percent. Having earlier won municipal elections in Bethlehem and Qalqilya, Hamas is now established as a political force on the West Bank, where Israeli security forces thought they had uprooted most of the organization's leadership structure, providing a complement to its even stronger position in Gaza. The *New York Times* described public reaction in two big cities: "In Nablus, thousands of Hamas members and supporters gathered in the city center chanting 'God is great.' The crowd carried the new mayor of the city, Ali Yaish—the wealthy owner of a Mercedes dealership—on their shoulders. In Jenin, marchers held up copies of the Koran and chanted, 'To Jerusalem we march, martyrs by the millions.'"[24]

A harbinger of things to come for Abu Mazen occurred just before dawn on September 5, when a convoy of about twenty vehicles armed with assault rifles and anti-tank grenades attacked the Gaza home of Major General Mousa Arafat, head of Palestinian Public Security Service in the Gaza Strip and a cousin of the late Yasser. Following a gunfight with Arafat's bodyguards, the intruders hauled the general outside in his pajamas and pumped thirteen bullets into his body and one into his head. The word was they were punishing his corruption.[25] The attackers were widely believed to be not from Hamas but from a dissident Fatah faction.

Gaza quickly became an advertisement for Abu Mazen's weakness as militias representing political factions, gangs, clans, or ad hoc bands of the criminally unemployed ran wild. Many were seeking and obtaining jobs with the PA SF; others simply had their names added to the PA employment rolls despite the fact that Abu Mazen had been warned his actions were bankrupting the government and discouraging foreign assistance. During the closing weeks of the campaign the United States dumped a reported $1.9 million into "short-term projects" for potential Abu Mazen supporters, but it proved of little avail.

The December results augured poorly for Fatah's prospects in the legislative council elections held January 25. Abu Mazen committed a serious political blunder by discarding the results of a summer primary that had showed voters ready to reject the old

24. Steven Erlanger, "Hamas Surges In West Bank; Blow to Fatah," *New York Times*, December 17, 2005.

25. Steven Erlanger, "Arafat's Former Security Chief Is Killed by Gunmen in Gaza," *New York Times*, September 7, 2005; and Tim Butcher, "Brutal Murder of Arafat's Cousin Endangers Gaza Peace Pact," *Daily Telegraph* (London), September 8, 2005.

"Tunisia crowd" of former Arafat confidants in favor of younger, less demonstrably corrupt candidates. Now the younger Fatah loyalists—led by top security or former security officials Jibril Rajoub on the West Bank and Mohammed Dahlan in Gaza—moved to submit their alternative list designed to push the Abu Mazen ticket off the ballot, or to at least secure a compromise list of candidates.

The political insurgents placed the jailed Tanzim leader Marwan Barghouti at the head of their list, a move Abu Mazen quickly copied. Previously, Barghouti had mounted a campaign from prison against Abu Mazen's initial election as Arafat's successor but was persuaded that Palestinian unity was the highest priority at the moment and dropped out of the earlier race. Now Abu Mazen was on the defensive and seeking to compromise with the rebels in order to avoid splitting the Fatah vote. By late December the parties had reached agreement on a "compromise" list headed by Barghouti, a list where most of the compromising had been done by Abu Mazen.[26]

Barghouti was at the time of his "nomination" serving a total of five life sentences for plus forty years for his involvement in three terrorist incidents in which a total of five people had died. From his prison cell he sought to reach out to Hamas sympathizers by emphasizing their issues—corruption, political reform, making sure Israel pulls back from the West Bank and Jerusalem. "Hamas is not an alternative to the Fatah movement, but a partner," he proclaimed. "Partners in the field, partners in parliament."

But Hamas had something far more precious than Barghouti's political embrace: an electoral system stacked in its favor. In the contest sixty-six seats were divided on the basis of votes for the

26. To cite one source on the compromise: Matthew Gutman, "Fatah Members Warn of War within Party: Compromise List Described as Proof of 'Alzheimer-ridden' Leadership," *Jerusalem Post*, December 30, 2005.

national lists while in sixteen separate districts with a total of sixty-six seats also at stake voters could vote as many times as there were seats up for grabs. In these districts the disciplined Hamas ran only enough candidates to compete for each seat while Fatah members running against the official Fatah slate crowded the ballots with a surfeit of candidates, thus dividing the Fatah vote. The result: Hamas candidates won 44 percent of the vote but won 56 percent of the seats; Fatah candidates polled 42 percent of the vote but won only 34 percent of the seats.

As the top man on the Fatah list, Barghouti, of course, won election to the legislature. A total of fourteen members of the Palestinian governing body found themselves incarcerated on Election Day, including ten members of the winning party, Hamas. Palestinian apologists immediately began fueling rumors of untapped moderation up and down the Hamas hierarchy. But those in the Israeli mainstream weren't buying. To them the prospect of a Palestinian negotiating partner seemed ever more remote and proposals for unilateral disengagement ever more compelling.

8. Unilateralism's Future

ARIEL SHARON WAS no happy warrior when the Gaza withdrawal began on August 15, 2005, telling Israelis, "It's no secret that I, like many others, believed and hoped that we could hold onto Netzarim and Kfar Darom forever. But the changing reality in Israel, the region, and the world has forced me to make a reassessment and alter positions."[1] Sharon's reassessment was Israel's. He was the indispensable party to the change, not just because he was the resident prime minister, but because it seemed he would be the toughest to convince and convert.

As noted, he had initially opposed the wall and in 2003 had run against unilateral disengagement. He had been the "Mr. Bulldozer" of Israeli politics in the 1980s, the conqueror and defender of conquest in the 1960s and 1970s, the "retaliator" against Jordanian-backed terrorist incursions in the 1950s while still in his teens. Before being stricken he took his adopted cause out of the Likud Party and was moving "Forward" (Kadima). He had defended it at times with reason, at times with bluster, at times with the suggestion that it would now go into a state of suspended animation or possibly morph into the proposed Road Map talks. The latter talks were proposed with some fanfare in 2003 and were meant to conclude with the formation of a sovereign Palestinian state in 2005. But when the next Road Map session

---

1. Quoted in Meir Elran, "Domestic Effects of the Disengagement," *Strategic Assessment* 8, no. 3 (November 2005).

is held, it will be the first. And the election of a Hamas-controlled legislature augurs poorly for that.

Sharon and Gaza necessarily—and with some reason—invite comparisons to Nixon and China. The hard-thinking if gravely flawed U.S. president, like Sharon, represented the conservative if not belligerent end of the national security spectrum. He had been a beneficiary of support from the "China Lobby," which backed the Formosa-exiled Nationalist regime and resisted any suggestion that the United States recognize a government that actually ruled the better part of a billion souls. The lobby trusted Nixon and others like him to maintain the fiction that Formosa was China, just as the Yesha Council trusted Sharon to maintain the fiction that Gaza was Israel regardless of the numbers—eight thousand settlers compared with 1.3 million Palestinians.

But when Nixon did move, the idea was so long overdue that the policymaking elites quickly institutionalized it. Given the Sino-Soviet split, the opportunity for the United States to play détente with one party and normalization with the other was just too good to be cast aside when Nixon himself hit the skids.

Unilateral separation, on the other hand, begins with a disclaimer on both sides of the equation. It is not a very satisfying policy, only, given the current circumstances, better than war, negotiations, or doing nothing. It is rooted in what for many is the painful concession that the dream of Greater Israel is, now and forever, unobtainable however many victories Israel wins both on the battlefield and in the gray world of counterterrorism. And from the peacemaking standpoint, unilateral disengagement is at best less desirable than a negotiated agreement with the other side—if only one could find a representative of the Palestinian people capable of making the deal and then making it stick. Such an agreement would have substantial advantages over the do-it-yourself approach.

The first such advantage is recognition by the international community and, most likely, active support from parties in the region whose backing could make a profound difference, namely, Egypt, Jordan, and possibly Saudi Arabia. The Gaza pullback produced a harvest of diplomatic rewards. A partial evacuation of West Bank settlements will produce no similar windfall.

Second, a negotiated deal would contain provisions for cooperative enforcement, verification, and dispute resolution. In other words, negotiations could promote regional security and, by virtue of their cooperative nature, deepen ties among former adversaries

Third, it would address every aspect of the dispute and settle all outstanding issues, with the parties renouncing additional claims. This "end of conflict" scenario could spur a change in the narrative of all sides, perhaps beginning the journey on the long road toward mitigating pervasive historical and cultural animosities.

Fourth, there would be undertakings designed to build and maintain mutual confidence. Such could encompass, for instance, forbidding either party to enter any alliance hostile or threatening to the other while maintaining Palestine as a demilitarized state.

Fifth, there could well be provisions for third-party oversight or peacekeeping. Such a presence is not unheard of in the area, as the Multilateral Force and Observers (MFO) has demonstrated in overseeing the Sinai Accord between Israel and Egypt.

Finally, there would almost certainly be provisions to build upon the already thick network of trade and economic relationships by facilitating travel, reducing checkpoint delays, and encouraging tourism. This would foster peaceful relations among and between the *people* in the region, not merely between the governments.

The only reasonable, indeed the only conceivable justification for rejecting these benefits and opting for unilateral separation is the absence of a negotiating partner. Before the Hamas "tsunami" of January 2006, PA leaders declared their readiness to negotiate, so ready in fact that they could conflate the three stages of the proposed Road Map into a single grand step. No need to dismantle the apparatus of terrorism—Hamas had chosen to participate in democratic elections for the legislative council. The Fatah-PA vision continued: Hamas would win a substantial but minority bloc of delegates, after which it would ask for representation in the PLO proportionate to its share of the vote. It would receive those seats, but Fatah and its allies would extract a price, namely, the subordination of the organization to majority rule, a renunciation of terrorism, and the disbanding of its militia, perhaps through merger into one armed force representing the PA. Never mind that Abu Mazen had issued the same call—"one authority"—before the Gaza withdrawal began and was summarily dismissed by Hamas and the others. And never mind that in the run-up to election he could not keep hostile militia fire away from his police stations, his election facilities, or even his own house. Soon Hamas would be a part of government and thus have a stake in order and stability.

Or so it was claimed. Both Israelis and senior U.S. officials were skeptical. They argued that Hamas, strong even if in the minority, would most likely try to emulate its Lebanese patron saint, Hezbollah, which has used its militia to secure its place in the political arena and its political connection to insulate its militia from calls to disband. The upshot is a Lebanese faction out of reach of the law, and one which, due to its anti-Israeli zealotry, is capable of sparking a cross-border crisis at any time. Nor are the Israelis very big fans of funneling Islamic militants into the national militia. One senior administration official recalls Sharon's derisive term for the Fatah militias—"Security Terrorists." His successors are unlikely to view Hamas units with any greater enthusiasm.

The Hamas victory changed the above equation less than one

might have thought. Abu Mazen, appearing more pathetic by the hour, proclaimed himself ready to begin negotiations with Israel. But Israeli prime minister Olmert concluded an emergency cabinet meeting by emphasizing his country's unwillingness to negotiate with any government of which Hamas is a part. The United States emphasized its long-standing position that any party to talks must first recognize Israel, renounce terrorism, and disband its militia. At a White House press conference addressing Hamas' victory, Mr. Bush told reporters, "I don't see how you can be a partner in peace if you advocate destruction of a country as part of your platform. And I know you can't be a partner in peace if . . . your party has got an armed wing." European reaction was similar.

But the pressure to negotiate cannot be escaped indefinitely. When he visited Washington in late May 2006 to receive the administration's blessing for his unilateral withdrawal plan, Prime Minister Olmert encountered resistance to Israel's unilateral drawing of final borders and pressure to begin some sort of peace talks with Abu Mazan. Meanwhile the Fatah leader, searching for a formula that would get Hamas to endorse his commencement of talks with the Israelis, began hinting at a national referendum backing the start of such talks.

It seems highly unlikely the Israelis will be parsing Hamas pronouncements for nuances in style or tone. To them, if there is any lesson to be learned from the Oslo years, it is that ideology counts far more than tactical endorsements of the peace process. Oslo was process oriented. It assumed that bedrock issues would be resolved because they were scheduled to be resolved and because the parties would be meeting to resolve them. But when the "moment of truth" arrived at Camp David and Taba, the Palestinians were not prepared to surrender the right of return and the Israelis were not prepared to resolve the issue by putting Israel out of business as a Jewish state. Had the Palestinians been taken at their word all along, the talks would not have reached so disastrous an end simply because the parties would have avoided the talks altogether or anticipated the nonresolution and taken steps in advance to cushion the shock, or even to change the subject of negotiation.

Now it is Hamas which must be taken at its word. Its very charter commits the organization to Israel's destruction and the creation of a single Islamic state with nothing but dead Jews commemorating the former State of Israel. It explicitly endorses the Protocols of the Elders of Zion, blames Jews for both world wars, and celebrates the day when, in a final climactic battle, the Muslims will slaughter the Jews. Moreover, the Gaza withdrawal has done little to quench the thirst for Israeli blood. The period since the August withdrawal has been reminiscent in certain respects of the early days of Intifada 2. The Palestinian narrative links the pullback from Gaza to the armed struggle, just as that violent period of late 2000 was inspired by Hezbollah's role in the pullback of Israeli forces from Lebanon.

Once again a suicide bomber murders civilians, five this time, at a mall in Netanya. Weeks later, another bomber at a checkpoint near Tulkarm kills three, including one Israeli officer. Both incidents, a third that injured a score of civilians in Tel Aviv, and a fourth, which killed nine in the same city are attributed to the PIJ. The PA condemns the attacks but moves neither nerve nor muscle against the planners. Instead, after the first incident Israel launches an arrest raid in Nablus, a town that had voted overwhelmingly for Hamas in local elections, killing three terrorists. Now the terrorists strike again, launching one of their periodic missile attacks from their Gaza strip sanctuary toward the southern city of Ashkelon—a bigger if more distant target than the more familiar Negev town of Sderot. Ashkelon is also more inviting to the terrorists because it boasts an important power facility. And now, with northern former settlements, or at least the rubble from places like Dugit and Nissanit in their hands, the Palestinian reach is longer.

Five Israeli soldiers were lightly wounded in the Ashkelon attack. Israel fired back, killing one Palestinian bystander. Deputy (now Acting) Prime Minister Ehud Olmert warned that, "If the rocket fire on Ashkelon does not stop, there will be a very fierce response, and no option can be ruled out, including a ground option."[2] Within days Israel declared a strip along northern Gaza as a "no-go zone," trying to push terrorist missile battery operators out of range of Ashkelon. Mahmoud Abbas opposed Israel's move, telling reporters, "Israel has left the Gaza Strip and has no right to come back."[3] His top negotiator, Saeb Arakat, complained, "This buffer zone will create more problems than it will solve and renew the cycle of violence."[4] He acknowledged, however, that PA security forces "haven't done a good job in stopping the firing of these Qassams."[5] Meanwhile representatives of PIJ, the PFLP, and Fatah's own al-Aksa Brigades pledged to continue the shelling.

The cumulative effects of these and similar incidents make it hard, if not impossible, for the Israelis to address the so-called quality-of-life issues—ease of travel, transport of produce, release of imprisoned Palestinians, employment inside Israel—that would earn the PA some political points with Gaza and West Bank constituencies. James Wolfensohn, the former World Bank president who is the Quartet's emissary to the area, came with plans to create conditions needed to draw billions of dollars of outside

2. Ehud Olmert, "Israel Threatens Harsh Response, Possible Invasion to Stop Rocket Fire from Gaza, 12/23/05," 7 News, Miami/Ft. Lauderdale, Friday, December 30, 2005.

3. Nidal Al-Mughrabi, "Israel Fires to Enforce Gaza Strip 'No-Go' Zone," Reuters, December 28, 2005 21:42:03 GMT (Reuters Foundation).

4. Steven Erlanger, "Killed by Suicide Bomber at Checkpoint in the West Bank," *New York Times*, December 30, 2005.

5. Ibid.

investment to Gaza and the West Bank. Instead he discovered
what countless emissaries before him have observed: the unique
ability of the Palestinians to bring out the worst in the Israelis, to
the ultimate detriment of both.

Sharon at one point threatened to make it difficult for Palestinians to get to the polls on January 25 if Hamas remained on
the ballot, a threat he withdrew after Condoleezza Rice protested.
By late December, the Israelis were talking about refusing permission for those Palestinians residing in Jerusalem—where Israel
claims sovereignty—to vote, a step that could possibly have killed
the entire election. After a plea from Abu Mazen they desisted.
Balloting scheduled for July 2005 had already been kicked forward to January 2006 in order to give Fatah time to begin wield-
ing the amenities of office to its own electoral benefit. The voting
made it clear, however, that without Yasser Arafat—the "Old
Man"—at the head of Fatah, Palestinians increasingly viewed the
party leadership as old, out of touch, deeply corrupt, and badly
in need of the kind of generational overhaul only a period out of
office could provide.

The Israeli desire to see the January balloting postponed was
not the product of cynicism. As noted by Tsipi Livni, the minister
of justice who followed Sharon to Kadima, excluding terrorists
from both government and the negotiating table is not anti-dem-
ocratic, but rather a democratic essential:

> When the international community and the United States speak
> about a two-state solution and about democratization within the
> Palestinian state, the meaning is that the same rules that even
> Europe uses when it comes to elections in Europe will be im-
> plemented by the Palestinian Authority. And the meaning is that
> it is forbidden—any political group in Europe cannot be part of
> an election or cannot participate in an election if it uses or sup-
> ports terrorist activities or governments. And the same rules will

be implemented here. And Hamas has to choose between being part of the political process or being a terrorist organization.[6]

Ms. Livni—now Olmert's foreign minister—speaks with unusual authority on such matters. She is the daughter of a renowned fighter in Menachem Begin's pre-statehood Irgun militia, a terrorist organization by any honest standard. In June 1948, shortly after Begin had agreed with David Ben Gurion to integrate the Irgun into the regular IDF army, a cargo ship named the *Altalena*, previously purchased by Irgun, left Europe for Tel Aviv. Aboard were an intermingled group of one thousand refugees and Irgun fighters plus rifles, Bren guns, Bazookas, ammunition, and equipment. Begin had agreed to turn some of the cargo over to IDF but wanted to retain enough to outfit some thousand newly integrated Irgun troops in Jerusalem. Ben Gurion ordered the ship diverted to Kfar Vitkin where his commander, Dan Even, gave those aboard ten minutes to agree to turn all weapons over to IDF. After the deadline passed with no response, Even opened fire. The fight was resumed after the ship steamed to a position just off the Tel Aviv beach. Sixteen Irgun fighters and three IDF soldiers were killed. The supremacy of IDF and the other institutions of state had been painfully redeemed. One might describe the lesson as "one authority, one gun, one law."[7]

The incident has assumed epochal dimension over the years. Those who loved Begin and the Irgun recall it as a bloody betrayal of dedicated men. Others, however, see it as an example of the tough steps that sometimes must be taken to tame a recalcitrant faction and subordinate it to government political and military control once the moment has arrived where only one chain of command is acceptable. In this sense, it was a difficult and painful

6. Tsipi Livni, transcript of interview with author, Jerusalem, August 14, 2005.

7. Yehuda Lapidot, "The Altalena Affair," Jewish Virtual Library.

part of the growth of the Israeli state out of competing factions, yet one crucial to the emergence of the state as a coherent political entity.

Boaz Ganor, a keen student of terrorism, thinks an analogous time has arrived for the Palestinians. In talking with him nearly five months before the January election, he urged Abbas to launch a civil war against Hamas and the other terrorist organizations:

> We had a civil war before the creation of Israel, the Americans had a civil war, and probably the Palestinians will not have any other way but civil war before they create a state because Hamas and Islamic Jihad would never in my view dismantle themselves voluntarily. And there is no regime that can let Islamic radical opposition have weapons and munitions and terrorist capabilities as much as they want, even if they take part in the political game and have some representatives in the parliament.[8]

Israelis generally have little respect for a political leadership that lacks the courage or the resolve to bring to heel its freelancing terrorist militias. Arafat was no Ben Gurion and Abu Mazen is a pale shadow of Arafat. For different reasons neither has offered the Israelis a true negotiating partner.

Nor does Abu Mazen's weakness end with his inability to bring Hamas and the other militias to heel. Arafat's negotiating shadow is as present as his political shadow. Again Ms. Livni offered valuable insight: "My understanding is that Abu Mazen now, weak as he says he is, and at the beginning of creating something in the Palestinian Authority, cannot sign an agreement that Arafat refused a few years ago. It's too early." Ms. Livni also warned that negotiations that fail may carry a price far more dear than waiting for a more propitious moment to talk, stating, "the Palestinians are not those who say, 'Okay, this is not our expec-

8. Boaz Ganor, transcript of interview with author, Israel, July 26, 2005.

tation, let's do some more talking.' They use terror and Intifada to achieve more political gains. And this is something we cannot afford."[9]

One caveat to the above was offered by Khalil Shikaki at the Brandeis conference insofar as the polling data has changed over time. In Arafat's period with the Intifada, a majority of Palestinians viewed themselves in a life and death struggle with the Israelis. Yet by the fall of 2005, a majority favored compromise built on the foundation of the two-state solution. A skillful Palestinian leader might have figured out a way to chase his followers back to meaningful negotiations. Unfortunately, Abu Mazen lacked the moxie to exploit the opening.

Much of the above would likely have proven academic had the United States, for whatever reason, pressed Israel and the Palestinians into Road Map talks, talks that have appeared as stillborn from the outset. With its great ally demanding negotiations, the terrorism of Hamas and PIJ would have become less the excuse for not talking with the Palestinians, but more the excuse for Israel not talking about anything else. If the apparatus of terrorism is to be dismantled as the Road Map demands in Stage One, then the PA must show that it controls all militias and weapons, that terrorist leaders are tracked, apprehended, and punished, and that attacks against Israel are not tolerated. The PA must account for the training and discipline of its armed security forces, and it must respond to Israeli demands that it work in tandem with Israeli security forces as well as third parties when it comes to intelligence and other counterterrorism operations. Very early on the PA will have to show that the purpose of intelligence is to help authorities to track terrorists rather than to help terrorists track authorities. None of this would have been doable even before the Hamas legislative council victory. An effort to

9. Interview with Tsipi Livni.

initiate such talks with the terrorist group in control of the government would be ludicrous. In this early period of uncertainty, however, one must keep in mind that the Hamas reign could be abbreviated by civil uprising, outside destabilization efforts, or a premature clash with the Israelis.

The Road Map and unilateral disengagement can be sequential rather than mutually exclusive. And the Road Map is not a condition precedent to the next round of unilateral Israeli withdrawals, this time on the West Bank.

Should Israel decide to take the next unilateral disengagement step, it must then choose among a number of possible plans. One of the leading ones, reportedly backed by such past Sharon advisers as Eyal Arad and Eival Giladi, is to stage a large unilateral withdrawal from much of the West Bank. The principal reason for this "Gaza first" rather than "Gaza only" approach is that the Gaza withdrawal only began to address the issues of demography and democracy at the center of the policy debate; separating eight thousand Jews from 1.3 million Palestinians was a good start, but only a start.[10] The West Bank, not counting East Jerusalem and the city's immediate suburbs, still holds 2.5 million Arabs and only two hundred and twenty-five thousand Jews and is potentially ripe for a similar solution to the demographic problem. In his first Herzliya Conference speech as acting prime minister on January 24, 2006, Olmert seemed to suggest that his own West Bank withdrawals would have as their ultimate aim defining the borders of the Jewish state. As he bluntly stated, "Israel will maintain control over the security zones, the Jewish settlement blocs, and those places which have supreme national importance to the Jewish people, first and foremost a united Jerusalem under

10. See Yehuda Ben-Meir, "The Post-Disengagement Anguish," *Strategic Assessment* 8, no. 3 (November 2005). Also, BBC, "Militant 'End West Bank Truce,'" September 29, 2005, BBCNews.com. Available online at http://news.bbc.co.uk/2/hi/middle_east/4292448.stm.

Israeli sovereignty. There can be no Jewish state without the capital of Jerusalem at its center."[11]

Different advocates of continuing unilateral disengagement by closing West Bank settlements offer different formulas. The safest political step would be to begin with the dismantlement of the illegal outposts demanded by the Road Map and, independently, by the United States. It is a step Israel has clearly been witholding for the moment when either a show of good faith or one of reciprocity is called for. That is and continues to be a mistake. When the government itself not only tolerates but participates in the violation of its own laws, as was documented in the Sason study of illegal outposts, it loses much of the moral standing that is a democracy's ultimate asset.

Once the illegal settlements are gone, the question of "what next" comes to the fore. Some advocates of unilateral separation would take a modest bite out of the settlements in northern Judea before concluding with the closure of every settlement east of the fence line. Others, applying a concept of national security long since overtaken by events, would preserve the row of remote, lightly populated settlements along the Jordan slope and valley.

As no sane prime minister would conceivably take responsibility for dismantling a modern city of twenty thousand, Ariel would remain in Israeli hands—at least until later negotiations with the Palestinians—when it could make a good subject for a land swap with the PA. Efrata, part of the Gush Etzion bloc, would be kept along with all other Jerusalem suburbs. Some would exclude from potential settlement those parts of Jerusalem predominantly populated by Arabs, a move that could be accomplished with a relatively minor adjustment of the fence line while others

11. Ehud Olmert, speech presented at the Sixth Annual Herzliya Conference, January 24, 2006. Text of speech available online at www.israelnewsagency .com/israelolmertherzliyaconferencedisengagement48770124.html.

would save Jerusalem for later bargaining and regard it as a wholly separate issue.

Dan Schueftan, a leading student of disengagement, speaks for a consensus when he says he would disdain a claim of sovereignty over the area retained, anticipating adverse international community reaction.[12] On the other hand, one respected commentator urges an assertion of Israeli sovereignty on the condition (highly unlikely) that the United States would formally join in recognizing this expanded Israel.[13] The policy of the United States has for so many years been designed to get the parties talking face-to-face about final status that support for the unilateral Gaza withdrawal may come to be regarded as at most the product of special circumstances or, perhaps, an aberration.

Under any reasonable plan, the Palestinians would again inherit Hebron. Kiryat Arba would be shut down. Most of the ultraorthodox settlements—as opposed to the extreme religious nationalist settlements—would survive as they are located just east of the Green Line, adjacent to pre-1967 Israel. While a majority of settlements (seventy to eighty) would go, the majority of people, as residents of the biggest settlement blocs, would remain. This result was inherent in the proposal Ehud Barak offered at Camp David, implied by the Clinton Parameters, and even included in the Virtual Geneva Accord. It is hard today to imagine any workable scheme producing a different result.

The case for continuing along the path of unilateral separation includes both political and security factors. For one thing, it is supported by a hefty majority of the Israeli public. Sharon suffered only one political setback in his Gaza pullback campaign, a

12. Dan Schueftan, "Unilateral Disengagement," *Israel and the Palestinians* (London: Chatham House, 2005), p. 99. This again demonstrates the tension between the intra-Israeli and Israeli-international community reaction.

13. Hillel Halkin, "Israel after Disengagement," *Commentary* 120, no. 3 (October 2005).

May 2004 rejection of the plan by a sixty to forty vote among registered Likud party members. By shifting his coalition partners he won support by comfortable margins in all subsequent tests, with the exception of one internal political squeaker when Likud considered advancing the primary date. But when the Likud then voted against accepting three new members recommended by Sharon, he decided to end the game once and for all and form his own new party.

Because Israel's "new center" supported unilateral separation, Sharon's new Kadima Party got off to a flying start. Labor found a feisty little battler in Amir Peretz. At first blush he may appear an attractive coalition partner. Upon closer inspection, however, he may well turn out to be the most left-wing candidate on national security issues his party has ever fielded, one whose curiosity about unilateral disengagement will quickly be sated and who is likely instead to press for a negotiated giveaway game, not to mention a host of intellectually bankrupt social programs. Olmert would be well advised to keep his right-of-center coalition options alive lest he find his government perpetually under the threat of dissolution by a Peretz-led Labor partner.

Opponents of a West Bank pullback are not without ammunition of their own, including the spent rounds of rockets fired from the sanctuary of Gaza to Israeli cities in the Negev. To some extent they are already in a position to say, "We told you so." Abu Mazen proved too weak to take political advantage of the opportunity provided by withdrawal. Hamas has captured legislative power while those who launched snipers and suicide bombers against Israel have reaped credit for the withdrawal. They vowed to shower Israel with rockets aimed inside the Green Line and succeeded at least as was necessary to make their political point. National security foes of the Kadima approach suggest that had it not been for the Gaza pullback, IDF troops would have responded to the Gaza rockets with sweeps by ground forces.

Ehud Olmert and other Sharon loyalists say there are no restrictions against such operations should they become necessary. But clearly the pullback has had some unintended consequences. Maintain this policy in Gaza and you have a nuisance, Olmert opponents might argue. Transfer it to the West Bank and you have a disaster.

Again, the argument assumes that the withdrawals are a reward for good Palestinian behavior rather than a way to make bad behavior less threatening while divesting the country of a population it can never absorb and should not try to dominate. The settlements beyond the fence that would be abandoned do not promote Israeli security; they are a drain on it. It is the psychology of withdrawal rather than physical security issues that fuels the secular opposition. This will be particularly true once the fence is completed. Unable to penetrate this security barrier with any frequency, the terrorists will likely concentrate on the more remote, less protected locations. And if the terrorists fail to get the point, if they continue to embrace the idea that each withdrawal is simply an invitation to further armed resistance, there are crash educational courses—recall Operation Defensive Shield—that can be administered effectively. And unlike Gaza, the IDF could and would remain on the ground in much of the evacuated area, at least until the fence is completed in 2006 or 2007 and perhaps until the PA and the new Hamas government sort each other out. No Israeli withdrawal is irrevocable. Not an inch of territory would be abandoned to which the IDF could not return should circumstances warrant. What is irrevocable is retreat from the notion of Greater Israel, ground which should have been vacated long ago.

Before the Gaza withdrawal, many expressed concern about the impact of the operation on the IDF. The concern proved groundless and the IDF came out of the affair with an enhanced reputation. Its motto coined for the operation, "Sensitivity and

Determination," proved on point. Its Special Negotiation Teams proved no less adept at dealing with traumatized settlers. Casualties were light. Relatively few soldiers, even from the devout *hesder* units—including some whose rabbis urged noncooperation—opted out.

The claim that the West Bank will be more difficult because the affected settlers are more militant is true, but only to a point. What doomed the Gush Katif opposition was not a lack of militancy but a lack of numbers. Eight thousand settlers are roughly 10–15 percent of the number of settlers who would, under any reasonable withdrawal plan, face evacuation from the West Bank. The Gaza number was, of course, augmented by tens of thousands of West Bank settlers, particularly the religious Zionists who led the anti-disengagement movement from the outset and organized through the Yesha Council. Many members of this group, influenced by their rabbis, doubted the disengagement would actually occur or felt that, if it did, it would be so violent and destructive as to make repetition on the West Bank nearly unthinkable. This group—the religious Zionists—is now going through a great period of introspection. Understandably so: in the end, the Gaza withdrawal took all of six days while the pullout from four settlements in northern Samaria was accomplished in a single day.

Yehuda Ben-Meir reported in *Strategic Assessment* that the more senior members of this community are moving toward a consensus judgment that they cannot respond to their loss by disassociating themselves from the remainder of Israeli society. They have effectively lost their veto power over settlement policy both as a short-run step and as the potential end result of negotiations. This consensus is at least partly offset by the conviction of many religious youth, bruised and embittered by their first battle in the arena of national policy, that the cure for failed militancy is militancy of a more pure, focused, perhaps even violent nature. The group now plays derisive word-games with the name Yesha Council, calling it the Pesha (Crime) Council or even the Yeshu (Jesus) Council because of its alleged propensity for turning the other cheek.[14]

But the passion of religious Israeli youth could not this time be translated into sufficient Knesset mandates to halt Kadima's momentum, even though the Olmert slate did less well on March 28 than had been anticipated. When the votes were tabulated, Kadima led the field with twenty-nine mandates. Labor had nineteen, and a spin-off pensioner group picked up another seven. Shas captured twelve. The Likud finished with a miserable dozen seats, only one more than an ad hoc party of Russian émigrés led by a man named Leiberman. Olmert could have gone to the left or right to form his coalition. He went both directions at once. He had ensured that Kadima's triumph would carry with it a mandate to make decisive changes on the West Bank by unveiling, during the campaign, his plan to redraw Israel's permanent borders by 2010 through a series of unilateral acts. Essentially the plan involved keeping Gush Etzion, Ma'aleh Adumiin, and Ariel along with those parts of Jerusalem thickly populated with Jews. The plan would shut down scores of settlements, requiring the relocation of about seventy thousand Israelis residing in West Bank communities. The issue of security was left undefined. If the withdrawals create "permanent" Israeli borders, it is tough to see how the sort of robust military and intelligence operations favored by Avi Dichter—now a prized member of Olmert's cabinet—can continue to operate on Palestinian territory.

The right wing can continue to make trouble for Olmert through demonstrations, civil disobedience, and acts of violence directed against either Israeli security forces or, more likely, Palestinians. Hamas, militant in ideology will likely be constrained by low international regard, bad political relations with Fatah,

14. Ben-Meir, "Post-Disengagement Anguish."

and Israel's chokehold over its economy. Were the Hamas government to fall and a chastened Fatah to recapture political control, Olmert could face both international pressure plus pressure from his left-wing coalition partners to return to a negotiation mode to resolve the final status issues of borders, settlements, refugees, and Jerusalem. That day may be a long way off. Meanwhile, Olmert seems likely to attempt to exploit the irony of having more freedom of action with a radical Islamic group at the helm than would be the case under a more "mature" Fatah regime.

Still, the presence of a Hamas-led Palestinian Authority confronts Olmert with both security and political challenges. Handing substantial parts of the West Bank over to Hamas brings within easy rocket range of Tel Aviv, Jerusalem, and other large cities representatives of an organization that advertises its endorsement of armed resistance to Israel. To neutralize this threat, Olmert will have to retain a substantial Israeli security presence in the area, even if most of the settlements are closed. This could deprive Israel of much of the international credit its withdrawal would otherwise have generated and trigger domestic disputes as well.

The Hamas face to the PA also exacerbates problems Olmert would certainly have faced anyway owing to the wall-to-wall nature of his coalition, running from Labor on the left to parties representing Russian-born immigrants and religious interests uncommitted to withdrawal on the right. Any move to relinquish the West Bank to Hamas could cause the right-wing side of the coalition to crumble. Olmert could then face the choice of holding new elections or seeking the backing of Arab Knesset factions in order to remain in office, a move that could tear asunder Israeli political society. Strong backing in the polls could save Olmert this choice as it did Sharon; as long as the polls remain in his favor Olmert will search for ways to play that card again and again.

He is likely to move quickly in an effort to have his borders fixed while the Bush administration remains in office. When determining the nations needed to satisfy their definition of "international recognition," the Israeli count goes no higher than the number one.

Index

Abbas, Mahmoud, xiv, 120, 147, 150; as prime minister, 32–33; retaliation and, 8. *See also* Mazen, Abu

Abdul-Karim, Qais, 60

Abdullah II, 130

Abrams, Elliott, 44

accords, Camp David, 43, 64, 120, 154; "land for peace," 42, 102; Wye, 124. *See also* Oslo Accords; Virtual Peace Accord (Geneva)

"adverse possession," 104

Agha, Hussein, 59–60

agriculture, 3, 13, 103, 112

Aliyah, 99

Allon Plan, 106

Allon, Yigal, 106–7

Al-Mujamma Al-Islami (Islamic Association), 79

Alrahman, Ahmad Abd, 62–64, 90–91

Altalena, 149

American Middle East Policy, 145

Amidror, Yaakov, 48

Annan, Kofi, 127

annexation, 71, 106; creeping, 29; of West Bank, 69

anti-Semitism, 12

anti-terrorist campaign, 48, 52, 84, 94, 126, 130

al-Aqsa Brigade, 26, 37, 54, 86, 90; activities of, 88–89; founding of, 88

aquifer, 13

Arab League Summit, 102

The Arab Times, 127

Arad, Eyal, 152

Arafat, Mousa, 138

Arafat, Yasser, xiv, 21, 26, 37, 43, 64–65, 67, 79, 150; Abbas and, 32–33; compromise and, 23; death of, 60; exile of, 59; Fatah and, 80, 121; fears of, 93; leverage of, 83; militias of, 87; negotiations and, 56; as "Old Man," 60, 148; as PA head, 80–81, 121; PLO and, 121; terrorists and, 38, 82

Arakat, Saeb, 147

Ariel, 55, 74, 117, 158; expansion of, 107; future of, 153; as Palestinian territory, 109; size of, 100; as West Bank settlement, 99

Arieli, Shaul, 18

Asad, Bashar, 44, 51

Ashwari, Hanan, 67–68, 74, 97–98

assassination, 86–87; of Rabin, 81; targeted, 94–95

Ayatollah Khomenni, 86

Barak, Ehud, 28, 45, 64, 107; ousting of, 23–24; as prime minister, 18

Barghouti, Marwan, 51, 87, 121, 139–40

Bar-Lev, Uri, 6

Bassiouni, Mohamad, 128

Bayit Leumi (National Home), 2

Begin, Beni, 42
Begin, Menachem, 36, 42–43, 104–5, 124, 131, 149
Beilin, Yossi, 21, 39
Beit Sourik, 71–73
Ben Gurion, David, 45, 124, 149–50
Ben-Eliezer, Binyamin, 28
Ben-Meir, Yehuda, 135–36, 157
Berlusconi, Silvio, 44
Betar youth movement, 42
Bezek, 52
blocs, 1, 11, 19, 40, 54, 100, 107, 117, 136; growth of, 109; Ma'aleh Alumim, 19; residents of, 154; settlers in, 109. See also settlements
blood libel, 77
bombings. See car bombings; suicide bombers
borders, xiv, 17–18, 51, 136, 159
breach of law, 5
breach of order, 5
Britain, 95
Burg, Joseph, 43
bus convoys, 123
Bush administration, 31, 35, 54, 83
Bush, George H. W., 23, 37, 44, 128, 136, 145; two-state solution and, 32; on UN resolutions, 54–55

Cairo Conference (2005), 129
Cairo Declaration (2005), 96
Camp David, 2003 talks, 23; Accord, 43, 64, 120, 154; failure at, 18; "moment of truth" at, 145; negotiations at, 107–8
"cantonization," 108
car bombings, 89
casus belli, 117
cease-fire (2003), 95
checkpoints, 6, 20, 37, 51, 59, 65, 87; civilian-manned, 75; delays

at, 143; Kissufim, 1; monitoring, 122; Rafah, 129
Chirac, Jacques, 125–26
City of Patriarchs, 117
civil disobedience, 158
Clinton, Bill, 18, 23, 64, 108
Clinton Parameters, 18, 21–22, 40, 109, 154
Cohen, Dudi, 5
collective farming, 3
Cook, Tsvi Yehudah, 2
corruption, 96
"creeping annexation," 29
Crown Center for Middle East Studies, 119
"cult of personality," 134
curfews, 37, 59

Dahlan, Mohammed, 63, 82, 139
Damascus, 79
Danino, Yohanan, 5
Da'wah, 79
"day after," 61, 90, 97, 124
Dayan, Moshe, 43, 102, 104
Democratic Front for Liberation of Palestine, 60
demography, 24, 26, 40–41, 65, 101, 135
demonstrations, 4, 6, 9, 158
Dichter, Avi, 41, 94, 158; on PA, 83–84; as security fence advocate, 27–28, 30; terrorism fatalities described by, 50–51
"draft positions," 22

E-1 project, 70, 110–11
East Jerusalem, 69–70, 116, 152
"eastern fence," 106
Efrat, 109, 153
Egypt, 128–29, 143
Egyptian peace treaty (1981), 11–12
Eitan, Michael, 24
El Al, 52
elections, 110, 120, 131; Fatah political party and, 96–97, 137,

140; Hamas and, xiii, 92, 96–97, 137, 140; of Mazen, 60, 121; Netanyahu and, 125
Eliyahu, Mordecai, 9
"end of conflict," 143
Erakat, Saeb, 64–66, 89, 94
Erdogen Tayyep, 126
EU. *See* European Union
European Union (EU), 19, 38–39
Even, Dan, 149
extremists, 57, 65

Fatah political party, xiv, 26, 37, 57, 60, 63, 78, 92; Arafat and, 80, 121; corruption of, 57; elections and, 96–97, 137, 140; Intifada treachery of, xiv; mature, 159; as Palestinian government, 86; Tanzim as offshoot of, 88; terrorism and, 85; viewed as "old," 148
Fatah Supreme Council, 87
Feldman, Shai, 119
fences, eastern, 106; smart, 68; temporary, 74. *See also* security fence
Force 17, 87
Fortune magazine, 52
Fourth Geneva Convention, 71, 74

Ganor, Boaz, 82–83, 150
Gaza, as dysfunctional, 14; escape from, 92; as Israel-controlled land, xiv; permanent residences in, 11; political situation in, 110; power struggle in, 97; pullback, 121–22; residents of, 12–13; returned to Palestinians, 15; security on, 93; settlements in, 1, 9, 11, 13; terrorists in, 95; unilateralism in, 119; withdrawal from, xiii, xv, xvi, 1, 3, 50, 57, 62–63, 125, 128, 134, 146
"Gaza first," 152
"Gaza only," 152

geography, 65, 135
Giladi, Eival, 27, 30, 152
GNP. *See* gross national product
Golan Heights, 2
Goldstein, Baruch, 105–6
Goldstein, Shaul, 15–16
government, of Fatah political party, 86; for Occupied Territories, 102; Palestinian, 86. *See also* Bush administration; Labor government
Greater Israel, 2, 25; advocacy of, 67, 124; dragon of, 117; dream of, 45; Green Line and, 25; notion of, 156; as Sharon legacy, 36; Zionism in, 42
Green Line, 54, 56, 72, 80, 103, 117, 124; Greater Israel and, 25; settlements near, 107–11
greenhouses, 10
gross national product (GNP), 103
Gulf War (1990), 80
Gush Emunim (Bloc of the Faithful), 107
Gush Etzion, 55, 110, 158
Gush Katif, 1, 5; battle to save, 6; evacuation of, 8; opposition, 157; terrorism in, 4
Gusha, Ibrahim, 85

Haaretz, 3, 6, 17, 35, 63, 101
hadith, 77
Hague International Court of Justice, 55, 74
Hajj, Ahmad, 96
Hamas, xiv, xvi, 14, 38, 48, 51–54, 60, 62, 70, 75–76, 90; charter of, 146; civil war against, 150; coherence of, 84; control of, 37; covenant of, 77, 80; in Damascus, 79; elections and, xiii, 92, 96–97, 137, 140; extremism and, 57; Mazen as subduer of, 61–62; military operations launched by, 84;

Hamas (*continued*)
  objectives of, 78; PA clashes
  and, 81; partners of, 85–86;
  politics of, 82; popular support
  for, 120; roots of, 77–79; Saraj
  on, 58; study of, 94; subduing,
  61; targets of, 80; undermining
  of, 95; U.S. and, 91–92, 145; as
  West Bank political force, 137
Hanegbi, Tzachi, 133
Haredi, 2
Harem al-Sharif (the Temple
  Mount), 20
Hassidim, 2–3
Hebron, 104–5, 154
Herut Party, 36, 42
Herzliya Conference, 35, 152
hesder yeshivot (religious schools),
  3–4, 157
Hezbollah, 28, 119, 144, 146
Histadrut union, 131
Holtzman, Shmuel Yosef, 103
home demolitions, 94
Homesh, 46
hostages, 7
human rights, 70
Hussein, Saddam, 51, 107

ICJ. *See* International Court of
  Justice
identity, 3
IDF. *See* Israeli Defense Force
IF. *See* Israeli Forces
industry, 13
Indyk, Martin, 29
informers, 51
Institute of Jewish Studies, 3
International Court of Justice (ICJ),
  70–71
International Policy Institute for
  Counter-Terrorism, 82
interrogation, 51
Intifada, 44, 85, 111, 117, 120,
  123, 128, 131, 134, 146; armed,
  59; First, 79; Jerusalem and,

111; for political gains, 151;
  products of, 61; Second, xiv,
  13–14, 18, 23, 32–33, 37, 58,
  82, 84, 88–89, 92–94, 96, 100;
  treachery of, xiv; waging of, 77
Iraq, 51, 107
Irgun militia, 149
Islamic Caliphate, 78
Islamic fundamentalist state, 97
Islamic Jihad, 52, 54
Islamic Resistance Movement, 77
Islamic University of Gaza, 79
Islamic values, 92
Israel, biblical, 72, 104, 107;
  expanded, 154; extinction of,
  78; fatalities from terrorism in,
  50–51, 50t; as Gaza controller,
  xiv; military of, 1, 3, 93; policy
  of, 135; political situation in,
  110; settlement of, 105; U.S.
  backing for, 66. *See also* Greater
  Israel
Israeli Defense Force (IDF), 1, 3–4,
  6–7, 9, 14, 27, 48; capabilities
  of, 49; defense against, 15;
  motto of, 156; protection by,
  105; redeployment of, 35; as
  settlement rescuer, 41; troops
  of, 100
Israeli Forces (IF), 93
Israeli National Security, 35
Israeli Supreme Court, 71–74
Israelis, xiv, 3
Izz al-Din al-Qassam squads, 84

Jabotinsky, Vladmir, 124
Jaffee Center for Strategic Studies,
  48, 119
Jennings, Peter, 67
Jericho, 64, 66
Jerusalem, 17, 159; Intifada and,
  111; "Old City" of, 20; as "open
  city," 20; wall, 9. *See also* East
  Jerusalem
Jerusalem Post, 14, 52, 119

Jews, French, 125; numbers of, xiv. *See also* Hassidim; Zionism; Zionists
Jihad, 79–80; global, 86; of Palestine, 86. *See also* Islamic Jihad; Palestinian Islamic Jihad
Jordan, 58, 101, 103, 130, 143
Judea, 1, 153

Kadim, 46
Kadima Party, xvi, 42, 50, 132, 141; halt of, 158; start of, 155
Karadi, Moshe, 5
Karni crossing, 122–23
Kasuri, Khurghid, 126
Katz, Yisrael, 107
Kfar Darom, 11, 49
kibbutzim, 3, 106
kidnappings, 89
Kiryat Arba, 104, 154
Knesset, 39, 47, 132, 158; Gaza withdrawal favored by, 50; laws of, 41; mandates of, 23; members of, 42
knife attacks, 89
Kollek, Teddy, 41
Kook, Avram Yitzhak, 2
Kuwait, 127, 131

Labor government, 18, 23, 29–30, 56, 102–3, 106
Labor Party, 131, 155
"land for peace" accord, 42, 102
land swap, 21, 23, 40, 153
law, 62, 144; breach of, 5; interpretation of, 72; of Knesset, 41; of war, 73
Le Monde, 21, 59
Lebanon, 3, 28, 30, 119, 146
Levinger, Moshe, 8, 104
Likud Central Committee, 133
Likud Party, 18, 24, 28, 36, 47, 50, 53, 56, 82, 104, 132; conflicts within, 124–26; "Princes" of, 42; Sharon and, 133–35, 141
Lincoln, Abraham, 137

Livni, Tsipi, xv, 12, 42, 148–50

Ma'aleh Adumim, 55, 110, 158
Madhi, Ibrihim, 77
Malka, Amos, 27, 30
Malley, Robert, 59–60
Mandate Palestine, 22
Maoz Yam hotel, 4–5, 49
Maqadmeh, Ibrihim, 95
martyrs, 26, 75. *See also* al-aqsa Brigade
Mashaal, Khalid, 79
Mazen, Abu, xvi, 37, 59, 64–65, 68, 94, 97, 119, 126; appointment of, 95; election of, 60, 121; as Hamas subduer, 61–62; independent militias called by, 92; moderates and, 76; Netanyahu and, 53; weakness of, 120, 135, 138, 145, 150, 155
Meridor, Dan, 24, 28–29, 42
Middle East Report, 94
Migdal Eder, 103
militias, of Arafat, 87; independent, 92; Irgun, 149. *See also* Force 17
Ministry of Construction and Housing, 115
Mintzer, Adi, 4
Mitchell, George, 32
Mitzna, Amram, 31
Mofaz, Shaul, 133
"Moratinos Document," 19–20
Moratinos, Miguel, 19
moshavim, 3
Mubarak, Hosni, 32, 37, 128, 130

Nachman, Ron, 99–101, 108
Natan-Zada, Eden, 8
National Religious Party, 43, 135
National Security Force (NSF), 93
Negotiation Support Unit, 65, 67
negotiations, xv, 7, 26, 143–44; Arafat and, 56; at Camp David, 107–8; PA and, 85; for Road Map formula, 37

Netanyahu, Binyamin (Bibi), 81,
132–33; elections and, 125; as
finance minister, 51–53; Mazen
and, 53; as prime minister, 124
Neve Dekalin, 14
New York Times, 127, 137
9/11 terrorist attacks, 25, 31–32
Nixon, Richard, 142
"no-go" zone, 124
nonviolence, 68
NSF. *See* National Security Force

Occupied Territories, 43, 71, 79,
102; self-government for, 102;
settlements in, 103
Olmert, Ehud, xv, 41–45, 113, 116,
136–37, 145, 147, 158–59; as
acting prime minister, 134;
opponents of, 156; on political
change, 46; on West Bank
settlements, 46–47
"one authority, one gun, one law,"
62, 144
Operation Defensive Shield, 50,
156. *See also* Oslo Accords
Oslo Accords, 18, 28, 30, 33, 62,
94, 111, 121, 145; opposition
to, 80; period of, 87
outposts, 106, 115, 153

PA Security Force (SF), 82, 89, 93
PA. *See* Palestinian Authority, 57
Palestine, as demilitarized state,
143; as Islamic state, 78; U.S.
and, 60
Palestine Liberation Organization
(PLO), 78–80, 84–85; Arafat
and, 121; restructuring of, 96
Palestinian(s), xiv, 11; elites, 61–
62, 65; Gaza returned to, 15;
judgment of, xv; liberals, 97;
living areas of, 69–70; martyrs,
26; moderate, xvi; as peace
partners, 26; proportionality
and, 74; refugees, 56; security
fence and, 69, 74; villages of,

100–101, 107; violence against,
158; on West Bank, 116
Palestinian Authority (PA), 57–58,
77–78, 83, 95, 146; Arafat as
head of, 80–81, 121; armed
forces of, 151; capping numbers
of, 81; equipping of, 128;
fragmentation of, 135; Hamas
clashes and, 81; leadership of,
33, 63; negotiations and, 85;
Road Map formula endorsement,
92; security forces of, 89;
terrorists and, 84, 132; weapons
and, 81, 94
Palestinian Center for Policy and
Survey Research (PSR), 119
Palestinian government, 86
Palestinian Islamic Jihad (PIJ), 82,
90, 146; controlling, 37;
organization of, 86–87; as
terrorist movement, 38
Palestinian Legislative Council, 96
Palestinian Muslim Brotherhood,
78, 86
Passover, 17, 104
patrols, 51
peace, 75; advocates, 39;
movement, 24, 68. *See also*
Egyptian peace treaty (1981);
Virtual Peace Accord (Geneva)
Peace Administration, 18
Peace Now, 106, 109–10, 113
Peres, Shimon, 45, 81, 131, 133
Peretz, Admir, 131–32, 155
period of calm, 90, 124, 129
Philadelphi Corridor, 122;
controlling, 53; Sharon and, 45;
supervision of, 61
PIJ. *See* Palestinian Islamic Jihad
PLO National Covenant, 78
PLO. *See* Palestine Liberation
Organization
Powell, Colin, 40
prisoners, release of, 37, 61;
treatment of, 82

privatization, 52
proportional representation, 96
proportionality, local, 73;
    Palestinians and, 74; tests of, 73
protesters, 5, 14
Protocols of the Elders of Zion, 78
PSR. *See* Palestinian Center for
    Policy and Survey Research
pulsa denura, 49

Qalandiya, 75
Qualified Industrial Zones
    agreement (2004), 129
quality-of-life issues, 130, 147
Qureia, Ahmed, 37, 120

rabbis, 4, 49, 130, 157
Rabbo, Yasser Abed, 39
Rabin Square, 9
Rabin, Yitzhak, 70, 100, 113, 135;
    assassination of, 81; rabbis and,
    49
Rafah, 122
Rajoub, Jibril, 139
Rantisi, Abd al-Aziz, 95
Ravitsky, Avi, 3
Reagan, Ronald, 23
reform, 68, 95
refugees, 13, 17, 21–23, 159;
    formula for, 40; handout on, 66;
    Palestinian, 56; right of return
    and, 66
"religious revolution," 3
Rice, Condoleezza, 120, 122–23,
    148
right of return, 26, 53, 65, 82, 96,
    125, 130; as excuse for war, 16;
    historic injustice and, 67; policy
    for, 13; refugees and, 66
Riskin, Shlomo, 109, 110
Road Map formula, xiv, 35, 112,
    128; demands of, 153; EU and,
    38–39; framework of, 54, 55;
    jump-starting, 44–45;
    negotiations for, 37; optional
    phase 2 of, 38–39; PA

endorsement of, 92; phase 1 of,
    38; pressure to accept, 40;
    resurrecting, 54; Russia and, 38–
    39; stages of, 144, 151; talks,
    132, 141, 151–52; UN and, 38–
    39; U.S. and, 38–39
roads, 111
Roosevelt, Franklin, 135, 137
Ross, Dennis, 23, 64
Russia, 38–39

Sadat, Anwar, 42
Samaria, 1
Sa-Nur, 46
Saraj, Eyad, 57–59
Sason, Talya, 113–14
Saudi Arabia, 143
Schueftan, Dan, 26–27, 39, 154
"seam," 59, 72
security, 35, 38; forces, 89; on
    Gaza, 93; personal, 51; on West
    Bank, 93; zone, 59, 72, 152. *See
    also* Israeli National Security;
    National Security Force
security fence, xiii, xiv, 6, 27, 29,
    41, 59, 68–69, 100, 116, 132;
    completion of, 156–57;
    configuration of, 75; Dichter as
    advocate of, 27–28, 30; graffiti
    on, 74–75; as middle-of-road
    approach, 30; Palestinians and,
    69, 74; route changes for, 74;
    for self-defense, 71; Sharon and,
    31; support for, 28; as violation
    of human rights, 70; West Bank
    and, 69
"Security Terrorists," 144
security wall. *See* security fence
Sefardi community, 9
self-determination, 22
settlements, xiii, 17, 100, 159; Ariel
    as, 99; dismantling of, xiv; in
    Gaza, 1, 9, 11, 13; IDF as
    rescuer of, 41; illegal, 112–15,
    153; along Jordan Valley, 106;

settlements (*continued*)
   near Green Line, 107–11; in
   Occupied Territories, 103;
   policies for, xvi; role of, 3; West
   Bank, xvi, 46–47, 99. *See also*
   blocs; outposts
settlers, 99; in blocs, 109; homes
   of, 121; "public convenience and
   necessity" of, 101; West Bank,
   116
SF. *See* PA Security Force
shadids, 43
Shafi, Salah Abed, 10
Shaham, Nisso, 5
"shahid," 86
Shalom, Sylvan, 126
Shanab, Ismail Abu, 95
Sharon, Ariel, xiii, xiv, xvii, 1, 4, 8,
   12, 17–18, 23, 27–28, 30, 48,
   64, 107, 141; allies of, 41; as
   "Bulldozer," xvi, 36, 141;
   conclusions reached by, 135–36;
   demography and, 40–41;
   Greater Israel as legacy of, 36;
   illegal settlements and, 112–13;
   land and, 126; Likud Party and,
   133–35, 141; as minister of
   agriculture, 112; motives of, 62;
   Nixon, in comparison to, 142;
   Philadelphi Corridor and, 45;
   rabbis and, 49; as "retaliator,"
   141; security fence and, 31;
   stroke suffered by, 42, 54, 133–
   34; terrorism and, 31–33;
   unilateral disengagement
   embraced by, 35, 44, 51, 108;
   West Bank pullout and, 46
Shavit, Avi, 17
Shikaki, Khalil, 119–20, 151
Shin Bet, 27, 48, 50, 83–84
Shlomzion Party, 36
Shura Council, 96
Silwan, 112
Sinai, 2, 11

Six Days' War (1967), 2, 11, 29,
   102
skullcaps, 2
"smart fence," 68
smuggling, 45, 53, 122
Sneh, Ephraim, 18
soldiers, 4; devout, 157; hesder,
   14; women as, 7
sovereignty, 154
Sri Lanka, 51
State of Palestine, 71
Strategic Assessment, 48, 82, 157
strategy, xiii
suicide, 15, 28
suicide bombers, xiii, xv, 17, 25,
   30, 41, 43, 89; birth of, 80;
   strategic threat of, 72
Suileiman, Na'il, 17
Sunnis, 86
surveillance, 122
sweeps, 94
synagogues, 10

Taba, 18–20, 22–23, 39, 66, 109,
   128, 145
Tabeja, Yossi, 17
tahdiya, 62, 86, 129. *See also*
   period of calm
Tamil Tigers, 51
Tanzim, 51, 87–88, 90, 120;
   activities of, 88–89; as Fatah
   offshoot, 88; terrorism by, 87
"temporary" fence, 74
territories, 109; GNP of, 103;
   withdrawal from, 19. *See also*
   Occupied Territories
terrorism, xvi, 7, 26, 32, 37;
   combatting, 51; decline in death
   from, 51; Fatah political party
   and, 85; fatalities from, 50–51,
   50t; in Gush Katif, 4; for
   political gains, 151; rewards for,
   136; Sharon and, 31–33; by
   Tanzim, 87; victims of, 9
terrorists, xiii, xv, 14; Arafat and,

38, 82; in Gaza, 95; PA and, 84, 132; PIJ and, 38; routes of, 45. *See also* anti-terrorist campaign; 9/11 terrorist attacks; "Security Terrorists"
"third force," 57
"Three No's" resolution, 102
Tomb of the Patriarchs, 105
Torah, 10
tourism, 25, 143
training, 93
travel restrictions, 37, 59, 61, 123
Truman, Harry, 137
tsitsis, 1
Tunisia, 79
tunnels, 122
two-state solution, 32, 67, 75, 112, 151; Bush and, 32; lip service to, 26

UN Disengagement Observer Force, 143
UN Resolution 94, 21
UN Resolution 181, 81
UN Resolution 194, 66
UN Resolution 242, 19, 54, 85, 110
UN Resolution 338, 54, 110
unemployment, 13
unilateral disengagement, xiv, xvi, xvii, 27, 29–30, 42, 110; as central issue, 76; claims of, 65; continuing, 153; future, 136, 152; proposals for, 140; Sharon embracing, 35, 44, 51, 108
unilateral separation, 121
unilateralism, 65, 119
United Nations, 55, 85, 126–27; resolutions of, 19, 21, 54, 66, 81, 85, 110; "Road Map" formula and, 38–39
United States (U.S.), 28, 95, 125; Hamas and, 91–92, 145; Israel backed by, 66; Palestine and, 60; Road Map formula and, 38–39

values, Islamic, 92; of Zionism, 117
vehicles, 93
Vinner, Erez, 84, 86
violence, 4, 13, 19, 33, 62; efficacy of, 119–20; against Palestinians, 158; prolonged, 25
Virtual Peace Accord (Geneva), 39–40, 109–10, 154

war, call for, 76; against Hamas, 150; law of, 73; right of return as excuse for, 16. *See also* Gulf War (1990); Six Days' War (1967); World War I; World War II
weapons, 14, 94; laboratories, 83; PA and, 81, 94; smugglers, 45, 53, 122
Weissgan, Asher, 8
Weissglas, Dov, 8, 40, 44
West Bank, xiii, 3; annexation of, 69; Ariel as settlement on, 99; conquest of, 2; disengagement plan for, 90; Hamas as political force on, 137; location of, 1; military intelligence on, 84; Olmert on, 46–47; Palestinians on, 116; political situation in, 110; pullout, 46; security fence and, 69; security on, 93; settlements, xvi, 46–47, 99; settlers on, 116
Western Wall, 20, 23
Wolfensohn, James, 147
World War I, 78
World War II, 78, 137
World Zionist Organization, 107, 115
Wye Accord, 124

Ya'Alon, Moshe, 30
Yad Vashem memorial, 127
Yassin, Achmad, 95–96
Yassin, Ahmed, 79
Yediot Achronnot, 45, 133

Yesha Council, 2, 4–6, 9, 157–58;
    leaders of, 7; political moves by,
    47
yeshivot, 14
Yousef, Hassan, 91–92

Zinni, Anthony, 83

Zionism, 4, 78, 107, 115; doctrine
    of, 2; fervor of, 3; in Greater
    Israel, 42; movement, 24, 47;
    orthodox, 2; values of, 117
Zionists, xv, 2, 157
Zuhri, Sami Abu, 92